SONG OF A WOMAN'S SOUL:
A Book of Prayers

SONG OF A WOMAN'S SOUL

A Book of Prayers

Compiled by Miriam Mindeman

Harold Shaw Publishers
Wheaton, Illinois

ISBN 0-87788-822-1

Compiled by Miriam Mindeman

Cover design by David LaPlaca

Library of Congress Cataloging-in-Publication Data

Song of a woman's soul : a book of prayers / compiled by Miriam Mindeman.
    p.   cm.
    Includes bibliographical references and index.
    1. Women—Prayer-books and devotions—English. 2. Prayers. 3. Woman—Religious life. I. Mindeman, Miriam.
BV4527.S645 1998
242'.843—dc21

98-10676
CIP

03 02 01 00 99 98

10 9 8 7 6 5 4 3 2 1

Contents

Acknowledgments

Many thanks to Anna Trimiew and Harry Verploegh for their contributions to this compilation.

Grateful acknowledgment is made to the following for permission to reprint their works:

Prayers beginning "I said, / I'm lonely" and "Let the words of my mouth," from *God Is No Fool*, Abingdon Press, Nashville, © 1969 by Lois A. Cheney. Used by permission of the author.

Selection from "A Prayer for Our Daughters," from *Grit and Grace: Portraits of a Woman's Life*, © 1997 by Joy Jordan-Lake. Reprinted by permission of Harold Shaw Publishers.

"My House, My Home," by Anne Keith from *Homecoming*, © 1996 by Jim Keith. Reprinted and adapted by permission of Jim Keith.

"Hope" and prayer beginning "Lord God Almighty, All-knowing . . . ," reprinted from *Clues to the Kingdom* by Edna Hatlestad Hong, © 1968 Augsburg Publishing House. Used by permission of Augsburg Fortress.

"Love Letter" and selection from "Come, Lord Jesus!" from *The Irrational Season* by Madeleine L'Engle, copyright © 1977 by Crosswicks, Inc. Reprinted by permission of HarperCollins Publishers, Inc.

Selection from "De Noche" by Poh Lian Lim, taken from *Finding God at Harvard*, edited by Kelly K. Monroe. Copyright © 1996 by Kelly K. Monroe. Used by permission of Zondervan Publishing House.

"The Master Beggar," from *Selected Poetry of Jessica Powers*, edited by Regina Siegfried and Robert Morneau, © 1989 by Sheed & Ward, 115 E. Armour Blvd., Kansas City, MO, 64111. To order call 1.800.333.7373. Reprinted by permission of Sheed & Ward.

Prayer beginning "I am a vessel that is broken . . . ," © 1997 by Ruth Richardson. Used by permission.

Introduction

Women throughout history and throughout the world have recorded their longings, fears, gratitude, suffering, and praise to God in prayer. In the middle of their personal circumstances they have given voice to the hunger for God shared by all human beings.

Gathered here are hundreds of prayers from women as widely separated by time and circumstance as fourteenth-century mystic Catherine of Siena and Underground Railroad pioneer Harriet Tubman, nineteenth-century English novelist Jane Austen and helper of the poor Mother Teresa of Calcutta, concentration camp survivor Corrie ten Boom and an anonymous 1990s mother of two boys. Some in this collection have captured on paper their faltering cries of distress or doubt; others have recorded their thoughts and God's responses during periods of contemplation; others have written down prayers to be used corporately; and still others have composed poetry and hymn prayers—literal songs from the heart to God.

Reading the many ways these women turned to God, we can pray and meditate as well and deepen our own faith. Looking in the direction these prayers point us, we can discover more of the character of the God who loves us and listens to every song we sing from our soul.

Hungering for God

In a sense, all of our prayer is a hungering for God. We recognize with great relief, and sometimes with great fear, that there is more to reality than our own limited selves. And, even if we have trouble trusting that a loving God really listens to us, we desperately hope he does. We need God.

None other Lamb, none other Name,
None other Hope in heav'n or earth or sea,
None other hiding place from guilt and
    shame,
None beside Thee.

My faith burns low, my hope burns low;
Only my heart's desire cries out in me,
By the deep thunder of its want and woe,
Cries out to Thee.

Lord, Thou art life, though I be dead;
Love's fire Thou art, however cold I be:
Nor heav'n have I, nor place to lay my head,
Nor home, but Thee.

—*Christina Rossetti, 1830–1894*
"None Other Lamb, None Other Name"

≈

Speak, Lord, in the stillness,
While I wait on Thee.

—*Emily May Grimes, 1868–1927*
from "Speak, Lord, in the Stillness"

You know, Lord, how well You know, the years
when I didn't pray (or didn't think I prayed).
How could I pray to Someone whose very existence I doubted. . . . Yet all the while I was
hungering for You, groping to find Your hand
as I stumbled in the darkness of my needs.

—*Marjorie Holmes, 20th century*
How Can I Find You, God?

≈

I thirst for light, to know, to see, to possess, as
we shall see and possess in eternity. I thirst for
perfect sympathy and the tenderness that can
read souls, and for close and strong union in
Thee. . . . I thirst for immortality, that complete
blossoming of the soul that we shall know beyond this transitory world. I thirst for life, the
only Life, full and eternal, with all our affec-
tions recovered in the bosom of infinite Love.
O my God, I thirst for Thee!

—*Elisabeth Leseur, 1866–1914*
in *My Spirit Rejoices*

Come, O Love, O God, Thou alone art all my love in verity. Thou art my dearest Salvation, all my hope and my joy, my supreme and surpassing Good. . . . Thou art the thirst of my heart; Thou art all the sufficiency of my spirit. The more I taste Thee, the more I hunger; the more I drink, the more I thirst.

—*Gertrude the Great, 1256–1302*
The Exercises of Saint Gertrude

❧

Come, thou Holy; pour out in our dim lives the steadfast radiance of the Living Perfect.

—*Evelyn Underhill, 1875–1941*
The Golden Sequence

❧

A hot wind from heaven
blows through me,
searing my soul.
I hear the sound
of wheels,
an army of voices,
the clatter of hoofbeats.

The holy messengers have come:
I watch, I wait, I am ready . . .

Take me up, Lord!
Take me up.

—*Anna Trimiew, 20th century*
"Going Home" (based on 2 Kings 2:1-11)

❧

O my Lord, Thou wast in my heart, and demanded only a simple turning of my mind inward, to make me perceive Thy presence. Oh, Infinite Goodness! how was I running hither and thither to seek Thee, my life was a burden to me, although my happiness was within myself. I was poor in riches, and ready to perish with hunger, near a table plentifully spread, and a continual feast. O Beauty, ancient and new; why have I known Thee so late? Alas! I sought Thee where Thou wert not, and did not seek Thee where thou wert. It was for want of understanding these words of Thy Gospel, "The kingdom of God cometh not with observation. . . . The kingdom of God is within you." This I now experienced. Thou becamest my King, and my heart Thy kingdom, wherein Thou didst reign supreme, and performed all Thy sacred will.

—*Madame Jeanne Guyon, 1648–1717*
The Autobiography of Madame Guyon

❧

O, look on us,
Father above! in tender mercy look
On us, thy children! . . .
Father in Heaven! we have no help but thee.

—*Felicia Dorothea Hemans, 1794–1835*
from "We Have No Help But Thee"

❧

I said,
"I'm lonely
I need God
    How do I pray?"
And God said,
"You just did.
Here I am."

—*Lois A. Cheney, 20th century*
God Is No Fool

❧

God, of your goodness, give me yourself; for you are sufficient for me. I cannot properly ask anything less, to be worthy of you. If I were to ask less, I should always be in want. In you alone do I have all.

—*Julian of Norwich, c. 1342–1413*

❧

My period had come for Prayer—
No other Art—would do—
My Tactics missed a rudiment—
Creator—Was it you?

God grows above—so those who pray
Horizons—must ascend—
And so I stepped upon the North
To see this Curious Friend—

His House was not—no sign had He—
By chimney—nor by Door
Could I infer his Residence—
Vast Prairies of Air

Unbroken by a Settler—
Were all that I could see—
Infinitude—Had'st Thou no Face
That I might look on Thee?

The Silence condescended—
Creation stopped—for me—
But awed beyond my errand—
I worshipped—did not "pray"—

—*Emily Dickinson, 1830–1886*
"My period had come for Prayer"

❧

And now, Lord, for more! . . . Your gifts are not enough, unless you give yourself. Oh Lord, show me yourself!

—*Hannah Whitall Smith, 1832–1911*
The Christian's Secret of a Holy Life, edited by Melvin E. Dieter

❧

Thou who alone art the Beloved of my heart, Thy face is all lovely and Thy Heart all inviting; but my thoughts, alas! go wandering far from Thee. Come, O God of my heart, gather together my scattered mental powers and fix them upon Thyself.

—*Gertrude the Great, 1256–1302*
The Exercises of Saint Gertrude

❧

Lord, I have not even begun to be consumed with longing for Your Word. Create in me a hunger for Your ways. May my heart be satisfied with nothing else than Your presence and Your Word. "Whom have I in heaven but Thee? And besides Thee, I desire nothing on earth."

—*Cynthia Heald, 20th century*
Abiding in Christ

❧

O God, O God, give yourself. What is all the rest? . . . Dearest Lord, keep me as I am, while I live, for this is true content, to hope for nothing, to desire nothing, expect nothing, fear nothing.

—*Elizabeth Seton, 1774–1821*

❧

You, O eternal Trinity, are a deep Sea, into which the deeper I enter the more I find, and the more I find the more I seek; the soul cannot be satiated in Your abyss, for she continually hungers after You, the eternal Trinity, desiring to see You with light in Your light.

—*Catherine of Siena, 1347–1380*
The Dialogue, translated by Algar Thorold

❧

Lord, teach us—teach me, Lord, teach me more concerning your holiness. I feel my utter need of casting myself wholly upon you.

—*Miriam Wenger, 20th century*
in *Silver Thread: The Ups and Downs of a Mennonite Family in Mission (1895-1995)*, by Joseph C. Shenk

&

Hungering for . . .

As women we are friends, mothers, sisters, daughters, wives, co-workers, leaders, and followers who give voice to our many needs in God's presence. In doing so, we see more of the immensity and love of our heavenly Father, and we find our hungers met.

Hungering for Courage

❧

O merciful God, be Thou now unto me a strong tower of defence, I humbly entreat Thee. Give me grace to await Thy leisure, and patiently to bear what Thou doest unto me; nothing doubting or mistrusting Thy goodness towards me; for Thou knowest what is good for me better than I do. Therefore do with me in all things what Thou wilt: only arm me, I beseech Thee, with Thine armour, that I may stand fast; above all things taking to me the shield of faith; praying always that I may refer myself wholly to Thy will, abiding Thy pleasure, and comforting myself in those troubles which it shall please Thee to send me, seeing troubles are profitable for me; and I am assuredly persuaded that all Thou doest cannot but be well; and unto Thee be all honour and glory.

—*Lady Jane Grey, 1537–1554*

Help me to be more fully decided in all things, and not to confer with flesh and blood, but to be bold to take up and firm to sustain the consecrated cross.

—*Catherine Booth, 1829–1890*

❧

O Lord God, set us free from Madison Avenue, from Hollywood, from Wall Street; set us free from the Joneses; set us free from our own fear of being different in a society that expects us all to dream one Dream. Set us free to live before you lives becoming the Gospel, lives proclaiming the Gospel.

—*Mary Anna Vidakovich, 20th century*
Sing to the Lord: Devotions for Advent

❧

Lord Jesus, I thank you for your salvation. I want it to be mine. . . . Make me your loyal disciple, no matter how difficult. . . . Make me faithful, God, . . . whatever the cost.

—*Mary Wang, 20th century*
The Chinese Church that Will Not Die

❧

Words prayed while traveling alone in West Africa through terrain alive with leopards, snakes, and crocodiles

O God of Daniel shut their mouths.

—*Mary Slessor, 1848–1915*

❧

Not one time
have You failed me,
Lord . . .

—*Ruth Bell Graham, 20th century*
Sitting by my laughing fire . . .

❧

Hungering for Strength

&

O Lord, with whom are strength and wisdom, put forth your strength, I implore you, for your own sake and for our sakes, and stand up to help us; for we are deceivable and weak persons, frail and brief, unstable and afraid, unless you put the might of your Holy Spirit within us.

—*Christina Rossetti, 1830–1894*

&

Give me strength, Lord, for living this hard moment to Your glory. May I honestly be willing to pay the price that is my part of the whole.

—*Edith Schaeffer, 20th century*
Affliction

I could not do without thee,
I cannot stand alone,
I have no strength or goodness,
No wisdom of my own;
But thou, beloved Saviour,
Art all in all to me,
And weakness will be power
If leaning hard on thee.

—*Frances Ridley Havergal, 1836–1879*

&

Help me, Lord God, in my good resolve and in thy holy service, and give me grace this very day really and truly to begin, for what I have done till now is nothing.

—*Mother Teresa of Calcutta, 1910–1997*
The Mother Teresa Reader

&

Now come I, crawling back to you—battered, bruised and shaken, and ashamed it would take so little to dismount me.

I cannot bring myself back to sweetness in you. My soul is weakened. Please lend me your hand. I desire to feed of you again. But you must do for me.

This incredible tiredness. Yet I cannot sleep. Can you lift this awful mourning, Lord? I feel as though I could cry all the time. I feel as though my heart, or my spirit, was broken. Repair me, Lord. Somehow, please repair me.

—*Karen Burton Mains, 20th century*
Karen! Karen!

❧

I cannot say my faith is strong,
I dare not hope my love is great;
But strength and love to Thee belong:
Oh, do not leave me desolate!

I know I owe my all to Thee;
Oh, take the heart I cannot give;
Do Thou my Strength, my Saviour be,
And make me to Thy glory live!

—*Anne Brontë, 1820–1849*
from "A Prayer"

❧

Ah! Lord, for Thy mercy grant me grace to obey and fulfil Thy will, and let never my . . . enemies have any power to hinder me from fulfilling Thy will.

—*Margery Kempe, c.1373–c.1438*
The Book of Margery Kempe

❧

We rest on Thee—our Shield and our
  Defender!
We go not forth alone against the foe;
Strong in Thy strength, safe in Thy keeping
  tender,
We rest on Thee, and in Thy Name we go.
Yea, in Thy Name, O Captain of salvation!
In Thy dear Name, all other names above;
Jesus our Righteousness, our sure foundation,
Our Prince of glory and our King of love.
We go in faith, our own great weakness
  feeling,
And needing more each day Thy grace to
  know:
Yet from our hearts a song of triumph
  pealing;
We rest on Thee, and in Thy Name we go.

—*Edith G. Cherry, 1872–1897*
"We Rest On Thee"

❧

I am a vessel that is broken.
My many pieces lay at Your feet.
And I long for what You've intended.
But all I offer is frailty.
That's what You ask for—
You ask for weakness,
that in my weakness
Your strength can be known.
It's hard to understand;
Your ways aren't mine, but
if You want weakness—
take all of me.

—*Ruth Richardson, 20th century*

❧

How rigid and inflexible I am! I can overcome my own stubbornness only with the greatest difficulty. And yet, when I beg you for help, you seem to do nothing. Are you ignoring me on purpose? Are you waiting for me to take the thorns of sin from my flesh before you will assist me? Yes, I know I must dig out these thorns before they poison and destroy me completely. But I cannot do it without you.

—*Hildegard of Bingen, 1098–1179*
in *The HarperCollins Book of Prayers*, compiled by Robert Van de Weyer

&

Uphold my heart in thee, O God,
Thou art my strength and stay;
Thou see'st how weak and frail I am;
Hide not thy face away.

—*Anne Bradstreet, 1612–1672*

&

O Lord, protect us from ever trying to reach the lost in our human ability. Fill us—and keep on filling us—with your precious Holy Spirit!

—*Evelyn Christenson, 20th century*
A Time to Pray God's Way

&

Oh, my God, if the value of prayer were but known, the great advantage which accrues to the soul from conversing with Thee, and what consequence it is of to salvation, everyone would be assiduous in it. It is a stronghold into which the enemy cannot enter. He may attack it, besiege it, make a noise about its walls; but while we are faithful and hold our station, he cannot hurt us.

—*Madame Jeanne Guyon, 1648–1717*
The Autobiography of Madame Guyon

&

Hungering for Life

❧

Precious Jesus, I beseech Thee,
May Thy words take root in me;
May this gift from heav'n enrich me
So that I bear fruit for Thee!

—*Anna Sophia of Hesse-Darmstadt, 1638–1683*
from "Speak, O Lord, Thy Servant Heareth"

❧

Lord, enable me to respond to painful circumstances with obedience and faith. Teach me the joy of offering "a sacrifice of praise" to You. Let my lips be fruitful in giving thanks.

—*Cynthia Heald, 20th century*
Abiding in Christ

❧

God, grant us faith and courage to keep "hands off" and allow the new garden of Your planting to ripen.

—*Lottie Moon, 1840–1912*
adapted

❧

Thank You, Lord Jesus, that . . .
Your resurrection life
makes us fit for earth.

—*Jill Briscoe, 20th century*
from "Resurrection Life," *Heartbeat*

❧

Hungering for Guidance

❧

I ask You to deposit in my mind and heart the particular dream, the special vision You have for my life. And along with the dream, will You give me whatever graces, patience, and stamina it takes to see the dream through to fruition? . . . I want to trust You enough to follow even if You lead along new paths. I admit to liking some of my ruts. But I know that habit patterns that seem like cozy nests from the inside, from Your vantage point may be prison cells. Lord, if You have to break down any prisons of mine before I can see the stars and catch the vision, then Lord, begin the process now.

—*Catherine Marshall, 1915–1983*
Adventures in Prayer

❧

O, Lord, don't let Satan deceive me, make it plain to me . . . make it clear, so as to make me understand it, and I will obey Thee. Now, Lord, I wait to hear Thee speak to me, and tell me where to go.

—*Amanda Smith, 1837–1915*
An Autobiography: The Story of the Lord's Dealings with Mrs. Amanda Smith, the Colored Evangelist

❧

O God, You must be trying to get through to me on a *very* great lesson this time. I'd like to ask You to let up a bit. But in a deeper part of me, I don't want You to let up till I've learned completely. I surely don't want to have to relearn *this* one by going through *another* such time as this.

—*Carole Mayhall, 20th century*
From the Heart of a Woman

❧

My loving Saviour, I am in your hands. Do with me as you will. . . . Lead me in darkness or in light—only keep me trusting you!

—*Hannah Whitall Smith, 1832–1911*
The Christian's Secret of a Holy Life, edited by Melvin E. Dieter

❧

Dear God, show me the narrow path this new year—your way, your plan. Let me be a part of your healing to our world. I thank you for all— for life, for the pain of it and the joy. Keep me in your way. Help me not lose sight of what is eternal and real.

—*Dreama Plybon Love, 20th century*

❧

I do not ask for any crown
But that which all may win;
Nor try to conquer any world
Except the one within.
Be Thou my guide until I find
Led by a tender hand,
The happy kingdom in myself
And dare to take command.

—*Louisa May Alcott, 1832–1888*
written at age thirteen

❧

Thine for ever! Shepherd, keep
These thy frail and trembling sheep;
Safe alone beneath thy care,
Let us all thy goodness share.

Thine for ever! thou our Guide,
All our wants by thee supplied,
All our sins by thee forgiven,
Led by thee from earth to heaven.

—*Mary Fawler Maude, 1820–1913*

I resolve to keep God in my thoughts and heaven in my view; to trust in the Lord with all my might, and not to lean to my own understanding; to acknowledge God in all my ways, humbly trusting that He will by grace and goodness direct my paths. These, most gracious God, are the sincere resolutions of a heart truly desirous to do Thy Holy Will and to obey Thy commandments. Hear me, O God, when I cry unto Thee for the help of Thy Holy Spirit.

—*Sarah Kirby Trimmer, 1741–1810*
adapted

ë€

A mother's prayer

God of all wisdom, we thank you for the changes that time brings upon all of us: for growth of little children, for maturity that comes with the years. We would not have our children remain babes . . . physically, emotionally, intellectually, or spiritually. As this infant grows day by day into childhood and adult-hood, help me as mother to guide these little feet in the narrow path that leads to life.

—*Helen Good Brenneman, 20th century*
Meditations for the New Mother

ë€

Hope

Lord, I see, I see!
The Kingdom hope is not
    a silly grinning hope. . . .
The Kingdom hope is the
    stripped-of-all-earthly-hope hope
    —the hope which says:
        I find no hope in me;
        therefore I hope in thee for me.

—*Edna Hatlestad Hong, 20th century*
Clues to the Kingdom

ë€

O Lord, Jesus Christ, who art as the Shadow of a Great Rock in a weary land, who beholdest thy weak creatures weary of labour, weary of pleasure, weary of hope deferred, weary of self; in thine abundant compassion, and fellow feeling with us, and unutterable tenderness, bring us, we pray thee, unto thy rest.

—*Christina Rossetti, 1830–1894*

৵

All these broken bridges—
we have always tried to build them
to each other and
to heaven. Why is it such a
sad surprise when last year's iron-strong
out-thrust organization, this month's
shining project, today's
far-flung silver network of good
resolutions
all answer the future's questions with
rust
and the sharp, ugly jutting
of the unfinished?
We have miscalculated every time.

Our blueprints are smudged.
We never order enough steel.
Our foundations are shallow as mud.
Our cables fray.
Our superstructure is stuck together
clumsily
with rivets of the wrong size.

We are our own botched bridges.
We were schooled in Babel
and our ambitious soaring
sinks in the sea.
How could we hope to carry your heavy
  glory?
We cannot even bear the weight
of our own failure.
But you did the unthinkable.
You built
one Bridge to us
solid enough, long
enough, strong enough
to stand all tides for all time,
linking
the unlinkable.

—*Luci Shaw, 20th century*
"Step on it," *Polishing the Petoskey Stone*

Lord . . . I am full of doubt and insecurity. . . . I feel bare and exposed—unsure of You and of Your love for me as an individual. . . . I feel alone and incapable of handling all that is required. I have lost the sense of Your presence, Jesus. How hellish it is.

Today, I choose, once again, to believe. In the void of my feelings and in spite of my doubt, I choose to believe in You, Christ my Savior. I will be a fool, if needed. No other options will do. You, Jesus, are my only Hope.

—*Dreama Plybon Love, 20th century*

❧

O Jesus! Love of my soul, You shall always remain to me, even though I should lose all else. . . . Yes, You shall remain, for You do not die, You change not and the fire of Your heart is as ardent as ever!

—*Concepción Cabrera de Armida (Conchita), 1862–1937*
Before the Altar, translated by Luisa Icaza de Medina Mora

❧

O glorious resurrection! God, in all the centuries during which believers have placed their hope in Thee, none has ever been deceived. Therefore my hope also is in Thee.

—*Ida Calvin, 1505–1549*
words prayed at her death, adapted

❧

I see the valley
  of the shadow of death
and I am not afraid.
You, Lord, are with me;
Your angels of mercy
  surround my bed,
and they comfort me.
I am ready for the journey
  through the stifling darkness
    to the open light beyond;
My heart is brimming with hope.

Surely goodness and mercy
  and the certain wings of angels
    shall attend to me,
and take me there;
then I will dwell in the home
  of the Lord
forever.

—*Anna Trimiew, 20th century*
"Psalm of Hope" (Psalm 23 adapted)

❧

O God, into Your hands I commend my spirit. To You I abandon my hopes and fears, my desires and repugnances, my temporal and eternal prospects. To You I commit the wants of my body; to You I commit the more precious interests of my immortal spirit.

Though my faults are many, my miseries great, my spiritual poverty extreme, my hope in You surpasses all. Though temptation should assail me, I will hope in You. Though I should sink beneath my weakness, I will hope in You still. I trust in You, for You are my God.

—*Frances Warde, 1810–1884*
in *Frances Warde* by Kathleen Healy, adapted

❧

God of the past and the present, I feel pain when I am forced to review my life. . . . I sit here in your presence holding a huge load of "if onlys." I cannot figure out what to do with them, and so I wait here for your good news that life can be different, that your holy presence can burst into my life and shatter my facade. . . .

If only, God, you would take my shattered dreams and put them back together. If only you could pick up the pieces of my broken hopes and make something out of whatever I have left. If only I could come to the end of my days having tasted the life-giving water of your spirit and having found the contentment to declare, "No regrets!" Help me, God.

—*Kathy Manis Findley, 20th century*
Voices of Our Sisters

&

Hungering for Peace

❧

Only in Thee
is stillness found.

—*Ruth Bell Graham, 20th century*
Sitting by my laughing fire . . .

❧

Dear Lord, whose mercy veileth all
That may our coming days befall,
Still hide from us the things to be,
But rest our troubled hearts in Thee.

—*Harriet McEwen Kimball, b. 1834*

❧

Let me neither look for nor find anyone but
You and You alone. Let all creatures be as nothing to me and me as nothing to them. Let no
earthly things disturb my peace. O Jesus, I ask
only for peace—peace and above all love that
is without measure or limits.

—*Thérèse of Lisieux, 1873–1897*
The Autobiography of St. Thérèse of Lisieux, translated by John
Beevers

❧

To the heart that knows Thy love, O Purest!
There is a temple, sacred evermore,
And all the babble of life's angry voices
Dies in hushed stillness at its peaceful door.

Far, far away, the roar of passion dieth,
And loving thoughts rise calm and peacefully,
And no rude storm, how fierce so e'er it flieth,
Disturbs the soul that dwells, O Lord, in Thee.

O Rest of rests! O Peace, serene, eternal!
Thou ever livest, and Thou changest never;
And in the secret of Thy presence dwelleth
Fullness of joy, for ever and for ever.

—*Harriet Beecher Stowe, 1811–1896*
from "When Winds Are Raging"

Please, God, may the flowers of peace bloom where there is now war or threat of war. May good will replace hate, and understanding end suspicion. In the name of the Prince of Peace.

—Josephine Robertson, 20th century
Meditations on Garden Themes

☙

Lord Jesus Christ, our God, the worries and cares of our lives beat up against us in great waves. Help us to see thee walking over the surging waters.

—Princess Ileana of Romania, 20th century

☙

Deep peace, pure white of the moon to you.
Deep peace, pure green of the grass to you.
Deep peace, pure brown of the earth to you.
Deep peace, pure grey of the dew to you.
Deep peace, pure blue of the sky to you.
Deep peace, of the running wave to you.
Deep peace, of the flowing air to you.
Deep peace, of the quiet earth to you.
Deep peace, of the shining stars to you.
Deep peace, of the Son of Peace to you.

—Fiona Macleod, 1855–1905

☙

Hungering for Understanding

❧

May I adore the mystery I cannot comprehend. Help me to be not too curious in prying into those secret things that are known only to thee, O God, nor too rash in censuring what I do not understand. . . . We are of yesterday and know nothing. But Thy boundless mind comprehends, at one view, all things, past, present, and future, and as Thou dost see all things, Thou dost best understand what is good and proper for each individual and for me. . . . So deal with me, O my God.

—*Susanna Wesley, 1669–1742*

❧

Lord, . . . Your ways are not our ways! And I am thankful that they are not. Your ways are higher—they bring You glory, they teach us about You, they make us like Christ, and they always have an eternal impact. Our ways are self-absorbed—they call attention to ourselves, they are designed to eliminate any discomfort, and they are focused on the immediate. To us, our ways seem best, and Your ways seem perplexing and hard. I know that trials are not optional while we journey here. Those who know You experience pain, and those who do not walk with You experience physical and emotional distress also. . . . In the world, there will be tribulation. But, Lord, what are You after? What do You want to accomplish with Your ways?

—*Cynthia Heald, 20th century*
A Woman's Journey to the Heart of God

❧

You are my understanding, and I shall know what it shall please you I should know. I shall not weary myself with further seeking, but I will abide in peace with your understanding, which holds possession of my mind.

—*Catherine of Genoa, 1447–1510*
The Life and Sayings of St. Catherine of Genoa, translated and edited by Paul Garvin

❧

Lord God Almighty, All-knowing, All-wise, Omniscient, Infinite, and Eternal One—I don't want crumbs and scraps of truth! I want the truth, the whole truth, and nothing but the truth!

God, when we humans have dealings with each other, when we want to affirm something as true, we give our word for it. That's all I ask, God—your word!

O Christ, how blind can I be! You were—you *are* that word! O Word of God, mystery revealed, truth made manifest, Word made flesh—and we crucified you!

—*Edna Hatlestad Hong, 20th century*
Clues to the Kingdom

❧

Seeking . . .

We remain seekers all of our lives, as we constantly return to God to ask for more light, more forgiveness, and more of his presence with us.

Seeking Light

❧

You loved me, without my having loved You. O Fire of Love! Thanks, thanks be to You, Eternal Father! I am imperfect and full of darkness, and You, Perfection and Light, have shown to me perfection, and the resplendent way of the doctrine of Your only-begotten Son. I was dead, and You have brought me to life.

—*Catherine of Siena, 1347–1380*
The Dialogue, translated by Algar Thorold

❧

You
are the One who put
stars
in apple cores

God
of all stars and symbols
and all grace,
You have reshaped
the empty space
deep in my apple heart
into a core of light
a star to shine
like Bethlehem's far-
to-near Night Sign:
bright
birth announcement
of Your
Day Star

—*Luci Shaw, 20th century*
"Stars in apple cores," *Polishing the Petoskey Stone*

❧

My prayers are lesser than three. . . .
Let me have light to see,
Let me have power to do.

    —Charlotte Perkins Gilman, 1860–1935
    from "Two Prayers"

❧

This day let Christ be risen in my heart,
That I may see Thee, Father, as Thou art.

    —Georgia Harkness, 1891–1974

❧

Bless'd art Thou, O Lord most high,
Who in Thy . . .
gracious love hast given
Light upon earth and light in heaven.

    —Alice Lucas, dates unknown
    from "The Night Prayer"

❧

Ever lift Thy face upon me
As I work and wait for Thee;
Resting 'neath Thy smile, Lord Jesus,
Earth's dark shadows flee.
Brightness of my Father's glory,
Sunshine of my Father's face,
Keep me ever trusting, resting,
Fill me with Thy grace.

    —Jean Sophia Pigott, 1845–1882
    from "Jesus I Am Resting, Resting"

❧

though
I am but dull wax
and a
dead wick
Lord, thou
wilt light my candle

    —Luci Shaw, 20th century
    "light my candle," *Listen to the Green*

❧

Father of mercies, in thy Word what endless
   glory shines!
For ever be thy name adored for these
   celestial lines.

Here may the blind and hungry come, and
   light and food receive;
Here shall the lowliest guest have room, and
   taste and see and live.

Oh, may these heavenly pages be my ever
   dear delight,
And still new beauties may I see, and still
   increasing light.

Divine instructor, gracious Lord, be thou for
   ever near;
Teach me to love thy sacred Word, and find
   my Savior
there.

     —*Anne Steele, 1716–1778*

≈

Let . . . thy light burn the mist from my
   mind.

     —*Avery Brooke, 20th century*

≈

O Everlasting Mercy . . . set us on fire, that
through . . . broken-hearted sinners your mercy
may banish the darkness and bring new life
upon the earth.

     —*Elizabeth Goudge, 1900–1984*
     A Diary of Prayer

≈

Youth Talks with God

Lighten the darkness of our life's long night,
Through which we blindly stumble to the day.
Shadows mislead us: Father, send thy light
To set our footsteps in the homeward way.

Lighten the darkness of our self-conceit,
The subtle darkness that we love so well,
Which shrouds the path of wisdom from our
    feet,
And lulls our spirits with its baneful spell.

Lighten our darkness when we bow the knee
To all the gods we ignorantly make
And worship, dreaming that we worship thee,
Till clearer light our slumbering souls awake.

Lighten our darkness when we fail at last,
And in the midnight lay us down to die;
We trust to find thee when the night is past,
And daylight breaks across the morning sky.

—*Frances Owen, 1842–1883*

&

I am your message, Lord. Throw me like a blazing torch into the night, that all may see and understand what it means to be your disciple.

—*Mother Maria Skobtsova, 1891–c.1945*
words prayed shortly after her arrest by Nazis for Skobtsova's aid to Jews in German-occupied France

&

Lord, make me like crystal that your light may shine through me.

—*Katherine Mansfield, 1888–1923*

&

Lord of life, beneath the dome
Of the universe, Thy home,
Gather us, who seek Thy face,
To the fold of Thy embrace,
For Thou art nigh.

While the deepening shadows fall,
Heart of Love, enfolding all,
Through the glory and the grace
Of the stars that veil Thy face,
Our hearts ascend.

When forever from our sight
Pass the stars, the day, the night,
Lord of angels, on our eyes
Let eternal morning rise,
And shadows end.

Holy, holy, holy, Lord God of Hosts!
Heaven and earth are full of Thee!
Heaven and earth are praising Thee,
O Lord most high!

—*Mary Artemisia Lathbury, 1841–1913*
from "Day Is Dying in the West"

You have led me through a thousand labyrinths
and enlightened my darkness. When shades
and perplexity surrounded me, my light has
broken forth out of obscurity and my darkness
has been turned into noonday. You have been
a Guide and a Father to me.

—*Elizabeth Singer Rowe, 1674–1737*

ॐ

Lord, have mercy on me. I need Your help in
recognizing where I am in danger of lighting
my own sparks and of rushing ahead to walk
in the light of my sparks instead of waiting for
Your help.

—*Edith Schaeffer, 20th century*
The Life of Prayer

ॐ

Come, Lord Jesus! Do I dare
Cry: Lord Jesus, quickly come!
Flash the lightning in the air,
Crash the thunder on my home!
Should I speak this aweful prayer?
Come, Lord Jesus, help me dare.

Come, Lord Jesus! Come this night
With your purging and your power,
For the earth is dark with blight
And in sin we run and cower
Before the splendid, raging sight
Of the breaking of the night.

Come, my Lord! Our darkness end!
Break the bonds of time and space.
All the powers of evil rend
By the radiance of your face.
The laughing stars with joy attend:
Come Lord Jesus! Be my end!

—Madeleine L'Engle, 20th century
from "Come, Lord Jesus!" *The Irrational Season*

Father, who the light this day
Out of darkness didst create,
Shine upon us now, we pray,
While within Thy courts we wait.
Wean us from the works of night,
Make us children of the light.

Savior, who this day didst break
The dark prison of the tomb,
Bid our slumb'ring souls awake,
Shine thro' all their sin and gloom;
Let us, from our bonds set free,
Rise from sin and live to Thee.

Blessed Spirit, Comforter,
Sent this day from Christ on high
Lord, on us Thy gifts confer,
Cleanse, illumine, sanctify.
All Thy fulness shed abroad;
Lead us to the truth of God.

—Julia A. Elliot, d. 1841

Lord, here we are, weak, much weaker than the devil of hatred. But Thou art stronger than the devil of hatred, and now we open our hearts to Thee, and we give thanks to Thee that Thou art willing to enter into our hearts, as the sun is willing to flood a room that is opened to its brightness.

—*Corrie ten Boom, 1893–1983*
Amazing Love

ða

In blazing light your cross reveals . . .
how great our debt to you.

—*Rosamond E. Herklots, 20th century*
from "Forgive Our Sins as We Forgive"

ða

Have mercy, Creator, on these Thy creatures. Reflect that we do not understand ourselves, or know what we desire, nor are we able to ask as we should. Give us light, Lord. Behold, we need it more than the man who was blind from his birth, for he wished to see the light and could not, whereas nowadays, Lord, no one wishes to see it. . . . Here, my God, must be manifested Thy power and Thy mercy.

—*Teresa of Avila, 1515–1582*
The Complete Works of St. Theresa, edited by E. Allison Peers

ða

O thou great Chief, light a candle in my
    heart, that I may see
what is therein, and sweep the rubbish from
    thy dwelling place.

—*An African schoolgirl*

ða

Be Thou my Vision, O Lord of my heart;
Naught be all else to me, save that Thou art.

—*Ancient Irish*
translated by Eleanor H. Hull, versified by Mary E. Byrne

ða

A Prayer for someone burdened by long-buried memories

Lord Jesus, I ask You to enter into this person who has need of Your healing in the depths of the mind. I ask You to come, Lord, as a careful housekeeper might come into a house that has long been closed and neglected. Open all the windows and let in the fresh wind of Your Spirit. Raise all the shades, that the sunlight of Your love may fill this house of the soul. Where there is sunlight there cannot be darkness. Therefore I rejoice that as the light of Your love now fills this mansion of the soul, all darkness shall flee away.

—*Agnes Sanford, 20th century*
The Healing Gifts of the Spirit

I want to gaze on You always and remain in Your great light.

—*Elizabeth Catez, 1880–1906*
Elizabeth of the Trinity: The Complete Works, translated by Sister Aletheia Kane

Rise in our spirits, O Bright Morning Star.

—*Twila Paris, 20th century*
from "Honor and Praise"

Seeking Forgiveness

❧

Eternal blessing be to you, my Lord Jesus Christ. In the agony of death, you gave to all sinners the hope of forgiveness when, to the robber who had turned to you, you mercifully promised the glory of paradise.

—*Bridget of Sweden, 1303–1373*
Birgitta of Sweden: Life and Selected Revelations

❧

Dear Lord, you see how we become used to everything. Once, we gladly took up your service with the firm intent of being wholly surrendered to you. But, since every day brings nearly the same thing over and over again, it seems to us that our prayer has been circumscribed. We limit it to ourselves and to what seems necessary for just the task at hand so that in the end our spirit has assumed the size of this small task. We ask you not to allow us to narrow ourselves in this way; expand us again.

—*Adrienne von Speyr, 1902–1967*
in *First Glance at Adrienne von Speyr,* by Hans Urs von Balthasar, translated by Antje Lawry and Sr. Sergia Englund

❧

If I understand aright, O Supreme and Eternal Truth, I am the thief and You have been punished for me.

—*Catherine of Siena, 1347–1380*
The Dialogue, translated by Algor Thorold

❧

I had better tell the truth since you know it already—I do not love you, O God; I love myself, my pitiful miserable self, well enough, and too well. My only comfort, my only hope is, that whether I love you or not, you love me and have sent your Son to seek and to save me. . . . Show your love to me by setting this wrong heart of mine right. Give me a clean heart, O God, and renew a right spirit within me.

—Hannah Whitall Smith, 1832–1911
The Christian's Secret of a Holy Life, edited by Melvin E. Dieter

❧

'T was thy child forgave the sin
Of the repentant Magdalen,
And blessed the thief on Calvary!—
Reject me not!

—Florence Earle Coates, 1850–1927
from "Suppliant"

❧

O thou King eternal, immortal, invisible, and only wise God, before whom angels bow and seraphs veil their faces, crying holy, holy, holy, is the Lord God Almighty. True and righteous are thy ways, thou King of saints. Help me, thy poor unworthy creature, humbly to prostrate myself before thee, and implore that mercy which my sins have justly forfeited. O God, I know that I am not worthy of a place at thy footstool; but to whom shall I go but unto thee? Thou alone hast the words of eternal life. . . . Be graciously pleased, O God, to pardon all that thou hast seen amiss in me this day, and enable me to live more to thine honor and glory for the time to come. Bless the church to which I belong, and grant that when thou makest up thy jewels, not one soul shall be found missing. . . . And now, Lord, what wait I for? My hope is in thee. Do more for me than I can possibly ask or think, and finally receive me to thyself.

—Maria W. Stewart, 1803–1879
"A Prayer for Purification"

My Jesus, forgive me, remember what thou hast done for me, and whither thou hast brought me, and for this excess of goodness and love let me no more hinder thy will in me.

—*Mary Ward, 1585–1645*
in *The HarperCollins Book of Prayers*, compiled by Robert Van de Weyer

❧

Just as I am, without one plea,
But that Thy blood was shed for me,
And that Thou bid'st me come to Thee,
O Lamb of God I come!

Just as I am, Thou wilt receive,
Wilt welcome, pardon, cleanse, relieve;
Because Thy promise I believe,
O Lamb of God I come!

Just as I am, of that free love
The breadth, length, depth, the height to
     prove,
Here for a season then above,
O Lamb of God I come!

—*Charlotte Elliott, 1789–1871*
from "Just As I Am"

❧

Lord, forgive me for what I said. I do not want to hurt Thy feelings with my self-pity. . . . Help me follow Thy leading, whatsoever Thou wouldst have me do.

—*Christiana Tsai, 1890–1984*
Christiana Tsai

I beseech the Lord, then, to deliver me from all evil for ever, since I cannot pay what I owe, and may perhaps run farther into debt each day. And the hardest thing to bear, Lord, is that I cannot know with any certainty if I love Thee and if my desires are acceptable in Thy sight. O my God and Lord, deliver me from all evil and be pleased to lead me to that place where all good things are to be found. What can be looked for on earth by those to whom Thou hast given some knowledge of what the world is and those who have a living faith in what the Eternal Father has laid up for them.

—*Teresa of Avila, 1515–1582*
The Way of Perfection

Be pitiful, my God!
No hard-won gifts I bring—
But empty, pleading hands
To Thee at evening.

Spring came, white-browed and young,
I, too, was young with Spring.
There was a blue, blue heaven
Above a skylark's wing.

Youth is the time for joy,
I cried, it is not meet
To mount the heights of toil
With child-soft feet.

When Summer walked the land
In Passion's red arrayed,
Under green sweeping boughs
My couch I made.

The noon-tide heat was sore,
I slept the Summer through;
An angel waked me—"Thou
Hast work to do."

I rose and saw the sheaves
Upstanding in a row;
The reapers sang Thy praise
While passing to and fro.

My hands were soft with ease,
Long were the Autumn hours;
I left the ripened sheaves
For poppy-flowers.

But lo! now Winter glooms,
And gray is in my hair,
Whither has flown the world
I found so fair?

My patient God, forgive!
Praying Thy pardon sweet
I lay a lonely heart
Before Thy feet.

—*Ethna Carberry, 1866–1902*
"Mea Culpa"

What to me may seem a treasure
But displeasing is to Thee,
Oh, remove such harmful pleasure;
Give instead what profits me.
Let my heart by Thee be stilled;
Make me Thine, Lord, as Thou wilt.

—*Ludamilia Elisabeth, Countess of Schwarzburg,*
1640–1672
translated by August Crull

❦

'Pears like, I prayed all de time, about my work, everywhere; I was always talking to de Lord. When I went to the horse-trough to wash my face, and took up de water in my hands, I said, "O Lord, wash me, make me clean." When I took up de towel to wipe my face and hands, I cried, "O Lord, for Jesus' sake, wipe away all my sins!" When I took up de broom and began to sweep, I groaned, "O Lord, whatsoebber sin dere be in my heart, sweep it out, Lord, clear and clean."

—*Harriet Tubman, c.1820–1913*
in *Can I Get a Witness? Prophetic Religious Voices of African American Women*, edited by Maria Y. Riggs

❦

Before the beginning Thou hast foreknown
   the end,
Before the birthday the death-bed was seen
   of thee:
Cleanse what I cannot cleanse, mend what I
   cannot mend,
   O Lord All-Merciful, be merciful to me.

While the end is drawing near I know not
   mine end;
Birth I recall not, my death I cannot foresee:
O God, wise to defend, wise to befriend,
   O Lord All-Merciful, be merciful to me.

—*Christina Rossetti, 1830–1894*
in *A Diary of Prayer,* compiled by Elizabeth Goudge

&

I have sinned, my God, and I am sorry. . . .
Pour the oil of your bountiful mercy on my
wounds, for you are my only hope; heal me.

—*Jeanne Frances de Chantal, 1572–1641*

&

Grant me your grace to forgive those who have
wronged me. Forgive me for not believing they
will change. I bring to you my self-righteous
attitudes. Enable me to taste afresh your complete forgiveness.

—*Rose Marie Miller, 20th century*
From Fear to Freedom

&

Lord God of Israel, hear our prayer:
There is no God in heaven above,
Or earth, that can with Thee compare,
Thou God of mercy, God of love!
Our fathers' God! O, hear us now:
Look down from heaven and bid us live;
Hear the petition, hear the vow,
And when Thou hearest, O, forgive!

Our Father, from Thy throne on high
Behold in love Thy people here;
Regard the contrite, humble cry,
The joy, the gratitude, the tear.
This temple, holy may it be;
Our offerings ever here receive;
And when our prayers ascend to Thee,
Our sins, our sins, great God, forgive!

Have pity, Lord, on all oppressed
With pain, anxiety or grief;
O, ever comfort the distressed
And to Thy captive grant relief.
Beneath Thy kind protecting wing
May we forever, ever live;

Hear Thou the offerings now we bring,
And when Thou hearest, Lord, forgive!

—*Mary Cutts, 1801–1882*
"Solomon's Prayer"

❧

I am truly sorry for my rebellion, O God. I pray that you will take it away and give me a radiant, compliant heart.

—*Anne Killinger, 20th century*
365 Meditations for Mothers of Teens

❧

Seeking God's Presence

Help me, Lord, to remember that religion is not to be confined to the church or closet, nor exercised only in prayer and meditation, but that everywhere I am in thy Presence.

—*Susanna Wesley, 1669–1742*

We know Thee, O Lord, our Redeemer; we know Thee in the breaking of bread; we meet Thee at the foot of the Cross; we meet Thee in the Garden in the sunrise.

—*Amy Carmichael, 1867–1951*
Rose from Brier

Open wide the windows of our spirits and fill us full of light; open wide the door of our hearts, that we may receive and entertain Thee with all our powers of adoration.

—*Christina Rossetti, 1830–1894*

Break Thou the bread of life,
Dear Lord, to me,
As Thou didst break the loaves
Beside the sea;
Beyond the sacred page
I seek Thee, Lord;
My spirit pants for Thee,
O living Word!

—*Mary Artemisia Lathbury, 1841–1913*
from "Break Thou the Bread of Life"

Dear Lord, she is so sick and I am so afraid. . . . My soul whispers, "Surrender, release her," and my mother heart cries in anguish "No! No, no. . . ." How can I lift her up to You of my own will? You could not need her as I do.

I am so weary and I cannot pray. . . . Nor can I hear You. My soul holds its hands over its ears and I bend away from the possible. . . .

I hope someone is praying for her, and for me. . . . Somehow I cannot find the courage to seek Your face and know the truth. . . . Not just now, please. Just stay close beside us, Your hand on my shoulder and Your love upon her.

—*Laura Margaret Evans, 20th century*
Hand in Hand: Mother, Child and God

ɞ

God to enfold me,
God to surround me,
God in my speaking,
God in my thinking.

God in my sleeping,
God in my waking,
God in my watching,
God in my hoping.

—*Traditional Celtic*

ɞ

I pray Thee with all my might, that Thou mayest not will to separate me from Thee. Thou well knowest, O Lord, that I could not bear this.

—*Catherine of Genoa, 1447–1510*
in *The Mystical Element of Religion as Studied in Saint Catherine of Genoa and Her Friends,* by Baron Friedrich von Hügel

ɞ

Sunshine let it be or frost,
Storm or calm, as thou shalt choose;
Though thine every gift were lost,
Thee thyself we could not lose.

—*Mary Coleridge, 1861–1907*
"After St. Augustine"

෧

Interject your voice, Father, above the noise of
the elevated train that rattles outside our windows, above the police and ambulance sirens
that whine toward the hospitals across the ex-
pressway. Insert your Presence above the
human anguish, the quiet desperation.

—*Karen Burton Mains, 20th century*
Karen! Karen!

෧

Out of my need you come to me, O Father,
Not as a spirit, gazing from on high,
Not as a wraith, gigantic in its outlines,
Waiting against the tumult of the sky!
Father, you come to me in threads of music,
And in the blessedness of whispered mirth,
And in the fragrance of frail garden flowers,
When summer lies across the drowsy earth!

Out of my need you come to me, O Father,
When I can scarcely see the path ahead—
It is your Hand that turns the sky, at
    evening,
Into a sea of throbbing, pulsing red—
It is your call that sounds across the marshes,
It is your smile that touches fields of grain,
Painting them with pale gold—it is your
    nearness
That makes me see new beauty, after pain!

—*Margaret E. Sangster, 1838–1912*
from "Recognition"

෧

O to continue to drink deep of the streams of the great salvation, until I wholly lose the thirst for the passing things of earth.

—*Ann Griffiths, 18th century*

❧

Though we forgot You—You will not forget us—
We feel so sure that You will not forget us.

—*Lucy Whitmell, 20th century*
from "Christ in Flanders," *The Spectator,* London, 11 September 1915

❧

I am come into a Presence.
passionate with patience
familiar as sorrow . . .
a space of mercy, a space of quiet
a dear and gracious place.

—*Poh Lian Lim, 20th century*
from "De Noche," *Finding God at Harvard,* edited by Kelly K. Monroe

Lord, grant us eyes to see
Within the seed a tree,
Within the glowing egg a bird,
Within the shroud a butterfly:
Till taught by such, we see
Beyond all creatures thee,
And hearken for thy tender word
And hear it, "Fear not: it is I."

—*Christina Rossetti, 1830–1894*

❧

O shine upon me, blessed Lord,
Ev'n for my Savior's sake;
In Thee alone is more than all,
And there content I'll take.

—*Anne Bradstreet, 1612–1672*

❧

Dear Lord, I know that without Your rest, I will not have strength for the journey, I will not enjoy the journey, and I will not bring You glory. I want to come to You and receive Your yoke, which enables me to receive Your rest and direction. I want to come before You in all honesty and say that my heart is not conceited and my eyes are not arrogant or pretentious. I don't want to be concerned about things that I can't understand; I want to trust You. I want to continue to grow so that I can come to You without demanding something in return. I want to know the joy and peace of Your presence. . . . I want Your rest.

—*Cynthia Heald, 20th century*
A Woman's Journey to the Heart of God

ॐ

Spirit of purity and grace,
Our weakness pitying see:
O make our hearts Thy dwelling place,
And worthier Thee.

—*Harriet Auber, 1773–1862*

ॐ

I pray that my heart will never become a stranger to you. Amen.

—*Elizabeth Larson, 20th century*

ॐ

Abide in me; o'ershadow by Thy love
Each half-formed purpose and dark thought
   of sin;
Quench, ere it rise, each selfish, low desire,
And keep my soul as Thine, calm and divine.

—*Harriet Beecher Stowe, 1811–1896*
from "Calm and Divine"

ॐ

Be the great God between thy two shoulders
To protect thee in thy going and in thy
  coming.
Be the Son of Mary Virgin near thy heart,
And be the perfect Spirit upon thee
  pouring—
Oh, the perfect Spirit upon thee pouring!

—Celtic Mother's Blessing, in *Carmina Gadelica, Hymns
and Incantations with Illustrative Notes of Words, Rites
and Customs Dying and Obsolete,* collected and
translated by Alexander Carmichael

❧

I see You, supreme goodness: your gaze is ma-
ternal.

—Mariam Baouardy, 1846–1878
in *Mariam: The Little Arab* by Amadée Brunot, translated by
Jeanne Dumais

❧

In losing all the gifts, with all their supports, I
found the Giver. In losing the sense and per-
ception of Thee in myself—I found Thee, O
my God, to lose Thee no more in Thyself, in
Thy own immutability.

—Madame Jeanne Guyon, 1648–1717
The Autobiography of Madame Guyon

❧

Speak to me low, my Saviour, low and sweet
From out the hallelujahs, sweet and low,
Lest I should fear and fall, and miss thee so
Who art not missed by any that entreat.

—Elizabeth Barrett Browning, 1806–1861
from "Comfort"

❧

If but my fainting heart be blest
With thy sweet Spirit for its guest,
My God, to thee I leave the rest—
Thy will be done!

—*Charlotte Elliott, 1789–1871*

❧

Lord, if I never feel your presence again, if I
never feel your love any more, if I never feel
that I want to help anybody, if I never want to
speak for you again, I commit myself to walk
by faith in obedience to your Word. I commit
myself to Jesus Christ without feeling.

—*Ruth Carter Stapleton, 20th century*
The Experience of Inner Healing

❧

Almighty God and Father of us all . . .
Look in your love upon us, your pilgrim
   people.

—*Sheila Cassidy, 20th century*
from "A Prayer," *Prayer for Pilgrims*

❧

Another year is dawning,
Dear Father, let it be,
In working or in waiting,
Another year with thee;
Another year of progress,
Another year of praise,
Another year of proving
Thy presence all the days.

—*Frances Ridley Havergal, 1836–1879*

❧

God of grave nights,
. . . of brave mornings,
. . . of silent noon,
Hear my salutation.

—Marguerite Wilkinson, 1883–1928
from "A Chant Out of Doors"

❧

You garment yourself in my soul, and my
soul is clothed
in you.

—Mechtild of Magdeburg, 1210–1294

❧

Christ, you are my house, my home—
A place, free to go out from
And return.
A place where, naked,
I can look in mirrors
And admit the flaws,
Knowing your mercy
Clothes the scars.

I have been lost in cities
Hours and days,
Breathless,
Searching for the roads
Unadvertised
That led me back
At last
To waiting welcome
And enfolding arms.

—Anne Keith, 1915–1994
"My House, My Home," *Homecoming,* adapted

❧

Marvelous Truth, confront us
at every turn.

—*Denise Levertov, 20th century*
from "Matins," *Poems 1960–1967*

≈

O sweet and loving God,
When I stay asleep too long,
Oblivious to all your many blessings,
Then, please, wake me up,
And sing to me your joyful song.
It is a song without noise or notes.
It is a song of love beyond words,
Of faith beyond the power of human telling.
I can hear it in my soul,
When you awaken me to your presence.

—*Mechtild of Magdeburg, c.1210-1294*

≈

O Lord God, as the heavens are high above the earth, so are thy ways above our ways, and thy thoughts above our thoughts. For wise and holy purposes best known to thyself, thou hast seen fit to deprive me of all earthly relatives; but when my father and mother forsook me, then thou did take me up. I desire to thank thee, that I am this day a living witness to testify that thou art a God that will ever vindicate the cause of the poor and needy, and that thou has always proved thyself to be a friend and father to me. O continue thy loving kindness even unto the end; and when health and strength begin to decay, and I, as it were, draw nigh unto the grave, O then afford me thy heart-cheering presence, and enable me to rely entirely upon thee. Never leave me nor forsake me, but have mercy upon me for thy great name's sake. And not for myself alone do I ask these blessings, but for all the poor and needy, all widows and fatherless children, and for the stranger in distress; and may they call upon thee in such manner as to be convinced that thou art a prayer-hearing and prayer-answering

God; and thine shall be the praise, forever.
Amen.

—*Maria W. Stewart, 1803–1879*
"A Prayer for Divine Companionship"

ช้

Abide in me, O Lord, and I in thee,
From this good hour, oh, leave me
   nevermore;
Then shall the discord cease, the wound be
   healed,
The lifelong bleeding of the soul be o'er.

Abide in me; o'er shadow by thy love
Each half-formed purpose and dark thought
   of sin;
Quench ere it rise each selfish, low desire,
And keep my soul as thine, calm and divine.

—*Harriet Beecher Stowe, 1811–1896*
from "Abide in Me, O Lord, and I in Thee"

ช้

God, I can push the grass apart
And lay my finger on thy heart.

—*Edna Saint Vincent Millay, 1892–1950*
from "O God, I Cried, No Dark Disguise"

ช้

Lord! Give me courage and love to open the
door and constrain You to enter, whatever the
disguise You come in, even before I fully recognize my guest.
   Come in! Enter my small life!

—*Evelyn Underhill, 1875–1941*
Meditations and Prayers

ช้

Longing . . .

Even if we begin with only a feeble desire to become like Jesus, we know that we can only do so by seeing all things—time, ourselves, our work, others—the way God sees them. Then, with his vision in us, our desire grows: we long to serve.

Longing to See with God's Eyes

❧

Lord, so attune my spirit to Yours that Your wayfarers, Your lost and lonely ones, Your needy and Your hungry and afraid, may never seek shelter at my heart in vain!

—*Margaret Clarkson, 20th century*
All Nature Sings

❧

This day which is now breaking should also belong to you. . . . It is still quite fresh, and it is as though anything could still be formed out of it. And we know that it is your possession. . . . In obedience to you we should make of it a chosen day, a space in which you can be at home at every moment and everywhere, a space which is filled by you.

—*Adrienne von Speyr, 1902–1967*
in *First Glance at Adrienne von Speyr,* by Hans Urs von Balthasar, translated by Antje Lawry and Sr. Sergia Englund

❧

God, patient of beginnings,
Help us . . . to see
In earthly bulbs, spring flowers; in man, the
   Christ;
In years, eternity!

—*Violet Alleyn Storey, 20th century*
from "A Prayer for the New Year"

❧

How does one of so few days
approach the Eternal One?
My days were always numbered,
The sun setting and the moon rising
marked them.
With every revolution of the Earth
my days diminished.
But you called me from my death march
and made an offer irresistible.
Not only have you extended to me
eternal life and peace,
but you replaced my way
with yours.

Why would any choose a countdown to death
when you are the way of life?
But death is mixed in with our pabulum
and covers us like skin.
And there is nothing so exquisitely charming
to the dying
than the day, the hour and the moment
of her death.
So we march to the end of the end
with
  No understanding

No peace
No way out.

Your way is of old, Lord.
Teach me to walk with you
in life eternal.
Then there will be no end,
No more beginnings.
The peace of such a way escapes me now.
But you have promised and
it will come to be.
And I will come to be with you.

"I AM" you call yourself.
Without you I am not.
Thank you for the peace
which comes from freedom.
Thank you for the days redeemed.
The sun rises with hope and
the moon sets with anticipation.
Grace marks my days
and Peace my hours.
The minutes belong to you
and the moments brim with life,
no longer death.

—*Caroline Scott, 20th century*
"To the Ancient of Days"

Let me not stumble blindly . . .
Just getting somehow safely through the
    days . . .
God—let me be aware.

—Miriam Teichner, b.1888
from "Awareness"

❧

Please remind me to live each day knowing I
will never live this day again.

—Doris W. Greig, 20th century

❧

I wonder, God,
If you had friends who were gods as well,
would they ask why you waste your time
on the skinned knees of a widow's grief
and the scheduling of human births,
instead of repairing cosmic tears
or writing more operas for angels?
And, would you answer

that they are all the same
Thing?

—Miriam Mindeman, 20th century

❧

Let me walk with you during every minute of
my life.

—Gemma Galgani, 1878–1903
from "Walking, Hearing, Watching, Dying, Rising," translated by
A. M. O'Sullivan

❧

Our days are numbered—let us spare
Our anxious hearts a needless care;
'Tis Thine to number out our days,
And ours to give them to Thy praise.

—Madame Jeanne Guyon, 1648–1717
translated by William Cowper

❧

Father, I know that all my life
is portioned out for me;
the changes that are sure to come,
I do not fear to see:
I ask thee for a present mind,
intent on pleasing thee.

I would not have the restless will
that hurries to and fro,
seeking for some great thing to do,
or secret thing to know;
I would be treated as a child,
and guided where I go.

I ask thee for the daily strength,
to none that ask denied,
a mind to blend with outward life,
while keeping at thy side,
content to fill a little space,
if thou be glorified.

In service which thy will appoints
there are no bonds for me;
my secret heart is taught the truth
that makes thy children free;

a life of self-renouncing love
is one of liberty.

—*Anna L. Waring, 1820–1910*
"Father, I Know That All My Life"

⁊

Every day Your mercy is brand new.

—*Twila Paris, 20th century*
from "I Never Get Used to What You Do"

⁊

God be merciful to me a sinner! I am deeply sensible that daily, hourly, and momentarily I stand in need of the sprinkling of my Saviour's blood. Thanks be to God, the fountain is always open; O what an anchor is this to my soul!

—*Lady Huntington, 1707–1791*
in *Lady Huntington and Her Friends*

⁊

I praise Thee while my days go on;
I love Thee while my days go on!
Through dark and dearth, through fire and
    frost,
With emptied arms and treasure lost
I thank Thee while my days go on!

And having in Thy life-depth thrown
Being and suffering (which are one),
As a child drops some pebble small
Down some deep well and hears it fall
Smiling. . . . So do I! Thy days go on!

—*Elizabeth Barrett Browning, 1806–1861*
from "Thy Days Go On!"

☙

Lord, shake away my indifference and insensitiv-
ity to the plight of the poor. . . . Show me how
I can serve you in the least of your brothers.

—*Mother Teresa of Calcutta, 1910–1997*
in *The HarperCollins Book of Prayers*, compiled by Robert Van de
Weyer

☙

Worse than the poorest mendicant alive,
the pencil man, the blind man with his
    breath
of music shaming all who do not give,
are You to me, Jesus of Nazareth.

Must You take up Your post on every block
of every street? Do I have no release?
Is there no room of earth that I can lock
to Your sad face, Your pitiful whisper "Please"?

I seek the counters of time's gleaming store
but make no purchases, for You are there.
How can I waste one coin while you implore
with tear-soiled cheeks and dark blood-
    matted hair?

And when I offer You in charity
pennies minted by love, still, still You stand
fixing Your sorrowful wide eyes on me.
Must all my purse be emptied in Your hand?

Jesus, my beggar, what would You have of
    me?
Father and mother? the lover I longed to
    know?

The child I would have cherished tenderly?
Even the blood that through my heart's
   valves flow?

I too would be a beggar. Long tormented,
I dream to grant You all and stand apart
with You on some bleak corner, tear-
   frequented,
and trouble mankind for its human heart.

—*Jessica Powers, 1905–1988*
"The Master Beggar," *Selected Poetry of Jessica Powers*

ॐ

O God of all history, help us to see the big picture—the whole sweep of time with which you are concerned—and to see our place in it. We are not the first or the greatest; we may not be the last. But we thank you that, even if we are the least, you still remember us and that your promises, your grace, your mercy are for us too.

—*Mary Anna Vidakovich, 20th century*
Sing to the Lord: Devotions for Advent

God, let me be conscious of it! Let me be conscious of what is happening. Let me realize it and feel it vividly. Let not the consciousness of the event (as it happens so often) come to me tardily, so that I half miss the experience. Let me be conscious of it!

—*Anne Morrow Lindbergh, 1906–1955*
prayed while driving to the airfield one morning, as recorded in her journal

ॐ

. . . All this new-born day, O Lord . . .
Let all its moments throb with joy.

—*Gabriela Mistral, 1889–1957*
from "Hymn for the Day," translated by James H. McLean

ॐ

Longing to Serve

❧

Surely Thou hast some work for me to do!
Oh, open Thou mine eyes,
To see how Thou wouldst choose to have it
  done,
And where it lies!

—*Elizabeth P. Prentiss, 1818–1878*

❧

I am grateful, Lord,
. . . that my busy hands
May move to meet another's need.

—*Janie Alford, 20th century*
from "Thanks Be To God"

❧

My blessed task from day to day
Is humbly, gladly, to obey.

—*Harriet McEwen Kimball, b. 1834*

❧

Dearest Lord, may I see you today and every
day in the person of your sick, and, whilst nursing them, minister unto you. Though you hide
yourself behind the unattractive disguise of the
irritable, the exacting, the unreasonable, may I
still recognize you, and say: "Jesus, my patient,
how sweet it is to serve you."

—*Mother Teresa of Calcutta, 1910–1997*

❧

God give me work till my life shall end and
life till my work is done.

—*Winifred Holtby, 1898–1935*

❧

O God! Here's me. Here's my Bible, here's my money! Use us, God! Use us!

—*Gladys Aylward, 1902–1970*
words prayed to offer herself again to serve God after she failed in Chinese language training and had to leave the China Inland Mission

❧

Let me be joy, be hope! Let my life sing!

—*Mary Carolyn Davies, 20th century*
from "A Prayer for Every Day"

❧

Bless, O Chief of generous chiefs
My loom and everything a-near me,
Bless me in my action,
Make Thou me safe while I live. . . .

Every web, black, white and fair,
Roan, dun, checked and red,
Give Thy blessing everywhere,
On every shuttle passing under the thread.

————

Bless, O God, my little cow
Bless, O God, my desire;
Bless Thou my partnership
And the milking of my hands, O God.

—*Celtic Blessings*
from *Carmina Gadelica, Hymns and Incantations with Illustrative Notes of Words, Rites and Customs Dying and Obsolete*, collected and translated by Alexander Carmichael

❧

Father God, may I be a healer in my family. May my spirit be one that unifies rather than divides.

—*Emilie Barnes, 20th century*
15 Minutes Alone with God

❧

God asks for my hands. Lord Jesus, here they are. Cleanse them and keep them clean for Thy use today.

—*Amy Carmichael, 1867–1951*
Whispers of His Power

❧

Let me work and be glad.

—*Theodosia Garrison, 1874–1944*
from "A Prayer"

❧

You are my Superior. I owe my life to you. I owe my meaning to you. You are my Source. . . . Help me to serve your will.

—*Priscilla Heidebrecht, 20th century*

❧

Lord, if You would appear to me and deliver me, that is just what I would like to do directly—try to help and comfort Your dear afflicted people.

—*Mary Grace Banfield, dates unknown*
From Death Unto Life: Diaries and Letters

❧

O Lord, may I be directed what to do and what to leave undone.

—*Elizabeth Fry, 1780–1845*

❧

Standing with Others

In front of us are so many who need us—family, friends, colleagues, people without God, people suffering grief or pain or poverty or homelessness or imprisonment or even torture. They need us to stand with them before God, to express their needs to him even when they cannot. And as we stand with them in prayer, we may see that God has given us opportunities and means to stand with them in other ways to relieve their burdens.

Incline us, O God!, to think humbly of ourselves, to be severe only in the examination of our own conduct, to consider our fellow-creatures with kindness, and to judge of all they say and do with that charity which we would desire from them ourselves.

—*Jane Austen, 1775–1817*

৵

Make us worthy, Lord, to serve our brothers and sisters scattered throughout the entire world, who live and die in poverty and hunger. Through the service of our hands, give them their daily bread; and by our understanding love, give them peace and joy.

—*Mother Teresa of Calcutta, 1910–1997*
The Mother Teresa Reader

৵

O Father Almighty, O sweet Jesus, most glorified King, will you be so pleased to come dis way and put you eye on dese poor mourners? O sweet Jesus, ain't you the Daniel God? Didn't you deliber de tree [three] chillun from the fiery furnis? Didn't you heah [hear] Jonah cry in de belly ub de whale? O, if dere be one seekin' mourner here dis afternoon, if dere be one sinkin' Peter, if dere be one weepin' Mary, if dere be one doubtin' Thomas, won't you be pleased to come and deliber 'em? Won't you mount your Gospel hoss, an' ride roun' de souls of dese yere mourners, and say, "Go in peace and sin no moah?" Don't you be so pleased to come wid de love in one han' and de fan in de odder han', to fan away doubts? Won't you be so pleased to shake dese here souls over hell, an' not let 'em fall in!

—*An Anonymous African-American Woman*
reported in *The Independent,* New York, 30 May 1867

৵

O God, Thou puttest into my heart this great desire to devote myself to the sick and sorrowful. I offer it to thee. Give me my work to do.

—*Florence Nightingale, 1820–1910*

ৰ

Let my children be committed to thy mercy.

—*Katherine von Bora, 1499–1552*

ৰ

It is a great torment, it is something almost inconceivable to one who loves you, the existence of all those people who do not know you, Truth so shining clear! Jesus, how is it possible! The soul cannot hold at the same time the deep knowledge of your Love and the thought of this world which is ignorant of you and seems to live without you. . . . Have pity on us.

—*Raissa Maritain, 1883–1960*
Raissa's Journal, presented by Jacques Maritain

May we strive to touch . . . the great, common heart of us all, and, O Lord God, let us forget not to be kind!

—*Mary Stewart, 1878–1943*

ৰ

We send up a cry of thanksgiving for people of all races, creeds, classes and colors the world over, and pray that through the instrumentality of our lives the spirit of peace, joy, fellowship and brotherhood shall circle the world.

—*Mary McLeod Bethune, 1875–1955*

ৰ

May every soul that touches mine—
Be it the slightest contact—
Get therefrom some good;
Some little grace; one kindly thought;
One aspiration yet unfelt;
One bit of courage
For the darkening sky;
One gleam of faith
To brave the thickening ills of life;
One glimpse of brighter skies
Beyond the gathering mists—
To make this life worth while
And heaven a surer heritage.

—George Eliot, 1819–1880
from "Making Life Worth While"

ᘓ

Enable me, O Lord, to feel tenderly and charitably toward all my beloved fellow mortals.

—Elizabeth Fry, 1780–1845

ᘓ

A mother's prayer

Jesus, Son of human mother,
Bless our motherhood, we pray;
Give us grace to lead our children,
Draw them to thee day by day;
May our sons and daughters be
dedicated, Lord, to thee.

—Emily L. Shirreff, 1814–1897
from "Gracious Savior, Who Didst Honor"

ᘓ

Prayer for a daughter

May [my daughter] never know hunger,
   material need; may she always thirst
for truth. Let her revere nature and in it
   find quiet, and reckless
communion with peace. May her passions
   have substance,
have heart behind words, not easily blown
   into heaps
by the breeze like bed sheets off the line.
   But her doubts,
may she face them and fearlessly test them;
   for belief is not blind,
nor faith without thought; no answer is
   injured by wondering why—
though the real cannot always be measured,
   nor the certain always seen.

   —*Joy Jordan-Lake, 20th century*
   from "A Prayer for Our Daughters," *Grit and Grace: Portraits of a Woman's Life*

ॐ

O God, You are the Healer . . .
the Hearer of your children's cries.

   —*Jill Briscoe, 20th century*
   from "A Prayer for Sick Children Everywhere," *Heartbeat*

ॐ

What heart can help breaking when it sees such dignity as Yours descend to such lowliness as our humanity? We are Your image, and You have become ours, by this union which You have accomplished with man, veiling the Eternal Deity with the cloud of woe, and the corrupted clay of Adam. For what reason?— Love. . . . By this ineffable love of Yours, therefore, I constrain You, and implore You that You do mercy to Your creatures.

   —*Catherine of Siena, 1347–1380*
   The Dialogue, translated by Algar Thorold

ॐ

81

May we offer his love outside of the boundaries of our own love. May we never let our hearts become so numb and so blind that we cannot see the face of Jesus in the people we meet in the everyday of our lives.

—Kathy Troccoli, 20th century
My Life Is in Your Hands

❧

I no longer shut myself away in my room, God, I try . . . to discover the small, naked human being amidst the monstrous wreckage caused by man's senseless deeds.

—Etty Hillesum, d. 1943

❧

. . . Let self be but a door
Through which young lives may come to
  Thee this day.

—Molly Anderson Haley, b. 1888

Dear Saviour, if these lambs should stray,
From thy secure enclosure's bound,
And, lured by worldly joys away,
Among the thoughtless crowd be found

Remember still that they are thine,
That thy dear sacred name they bear,
Think that the seal of love divine,
The sign of covenant grace they wear.

—Abby Bradley Hyde, 1799–1872
from "Dear Saviour, If These Lambs Should Stray"

❧

Teach me to love Thee in the passer-by.

—Nadejda de Bragança, d. 1946
from "Prayer"

❧

We thank thee for the courage of those who are called upon to lead and, in leading, to stand alone. Help us to appreciate the cost to the individual of those who renounce much to serve their fellow men, and may we, as we can, give them support. In the name of One who stood alone for all mankind.

—*Josephine Robertson, 20th century*
Meditations on Garden Themes

❧

Help us, O God, to do our best to help other people to accomplish and to achieve, knowing that their contribution is what God is trying to give the world.

—*Florence Simms, 1873–1923*

❧

God help the homeless ones who lack this night
A roof for shelter and a couch for sleep;
God help the sailormen who long for light
As restlessly they toss upon the deep.

God keep the orphaned children who are left
Unmothered in this world of chill and dole;
God keep the widowed hearts, of joy bereft;
God make all weary broken spirits whole.

—*Margaret E. Sangster, 1838–1912*
from "Midnight"

❧

In every human being, I love something of You.

—*Etty Hillesum, d. 1943*

❧

Holy Father, in thy mercy,
Hear our anxious prayer,
Keep our loved ones, now far distant,
'Neath thy care.

Jesus, Saviour, let thy presence
Be their light and guide;
Keep, O, keep them, in their weakness,
At thy side. . . .

May the joy of thy salvation
Be their strength and stay;
May they love and may they praise thee
Day by day.

Father, Son, and Holy Spirit,
God the One in Three,
Bless them, guide them, save them, keep
   them
Near to thee.

—*Isabella S. Stevenson, 1843–1890*

ఆ

Hear me, O loving Lord, according to the
sweetness of Thy paternal love, for her for
whom I pray.

—*Gertrude the Great, 1256–1302*

ఆ

O Lord, strengthen and support . . . all persons
unjustly accused or underrated. Comfort them
by the ever-present thought that you know the
whole truth, and will, in your own good time,
make their righteousness as clear as the light.
Give them grace to pray for such as do them
wrong, and hear and bless them when they
pray; for the sake of Jesus Christ our Lord and
Savior.

—*Christina Rossetti, 1830–1894*

ఆ

God keep you, dearest, all this lonely night:
  The winds are still;
  The moon drops down behind the western
  hill;
God keep you safely, dearest, till the light.

God keep you then when slumber melts away,
  And cares and strife
Take up new arms to fret our waking life,
God keep you through the battle of the day.

God keep you. Nay, beloved soul, how vain,
  How poor is prayer!
I can but say, again and yet again,
God keep you every time and everywhere.

—*Madeline Bridges, 1840–1920*
"God Keep You"

❧

Take from me all that hinders and teach me to accept in its place all that you accept: the ceaseless demands, needs, conflicts, pressures, misunderstandings even of those who love you best.

—*Evelyn Underhill, 1875–1941*

❧

I have confidence, my Lord, in these servants of Thine . . . knowing that they neither desire nor strive after anything but to please Thee. For Thy sake they have left the little they possessed, wishing they had more so that they might serve Thee with it. Since Thou, my Creator, art not ungrateful, I do not think Thou wilt fail to do what they beseech of Thee, for when Thou wert in the world, Lord, Thou didst not despise women, but didst always help them and show them great compassion.

—*Teresa of Avila, 1515–1582*

❧

Send whom thou wilt to kings and rulers of the earth, but let me be a servant to the servants of my Lord. Let me administer to the afflicted members of my exalted and glorious Redeemer. Let this be my lot, and I give the glories of the world to the wind.

—*Elizabeth Singer Rowe, 1674–1737*

⁊

My Father, take them, keep them for Thine own.

—*Katherine G. Howard, 1899–1987*
from "The Comfort of the Scriptures to a Mother of Six"

⁊

All this day, O Lord, let me touch as many lives as possible for thee; and every life I touch, do thou by thy Spirit quicken, whether through the word I speak, the prayer I breathe, or the life I live.

—*Mary Sumner, 1828–1921*

Oh Father, just send revival—any way, anytime, and with anybody. Just send it!

—*Evelyn Christenson, 20th century*
A Time to Pray God's Way

⁊

O Father of light and giver of all wisdom, bless every society formed for the advancement and spread of Thy truth, at home and abroad. Look with favor on all missionaries. Let Thy word have free course everywhere. . . . Give Thy servants health and strength, vigor of mind and devotedness of heart. . . . Grant that thousands and tens of thousands may rise up to call Thee blessed.

—*Hannah More, 1745–1833*

⁊

Suffering

In suffering, we appeal to One who suffered for us. For this reason, even when our agony is not eased, and even if we never find out the reason for it, we know that we are not alone and that God will bring all possible good from it.

To Thee I bring my care,
The care I cannot flee;
Thou wilt not only share,
But bear it all for me.
O loving Saviour, now to Thee
I bring the load that wearies me.

—*Frances Ridley Havergal, 1836–1879*

♥

Lord have mercy, Lord have mercy, Lord have mercy. Have mercy on the violence. Have mercy on the children. Have mercy on my weakness. Have mercy on my broken marriage. Have mercy on me.

—*Susan Hagood Lee, 20th century*
"Witness to Christ, Witness to Pain: One Woman's Journey through Wife Battering," in *Sermons Seldom Heard*

♥

I come down here, Lord, cause I ain't got no where else to go. I come down here knowing I ain't got no right, but I got a heavy need. I'm suffering so, Lord; my body is heavy like I'm carrying a stone. I come to ask you to move the stone, Jesus. Please move the stone!

—*Margaret Abigail Walker Alexander, 20th century*
Jubilee

♥

Must I now go on alone with You,
And is there no one near to hold my hand?

—*Evelyn Harris Brand, 1879–1974*

♥

I can no longer walk, can no longer work, can no longer choose for myself what I can sacrifice to you during the day. Sacrifice has taken on a different form now: I must simply accept everything and can only offer you always anew the desire that everything may take place according to your will. . . . I ask you to help me also in my weariness so that I may not tire of sacrificing everything to you. And bless this suffering for your whole Church and for all who seek the way to you.

—*Adrienne von Speyr, 1902–1967*
words prayed as an elderly woman in *First Glance at Adrienne von Speyr*, by Hans Urs von Balthasar, translated by Antje Lawry and Sr. Sergia Englund

ба

O Lord, remember not only the men and women of good will, but also those of ill will. But do not remember all the suffering they have inflicted on us; remember the fruits we have bought, thanks to this suffering—our comradeship, our loyalty, our humility, our courage, our generosity, the greatness of heart which has grown out of all this, and when they come to judgement let all the fruits which we have borne be their forgiveness.

—*written by an unknown prisoner and left near the body of a dead child in Ravensbruck concentration camp, where 92,000 women and children died*

ба

A dreadful darkness closes in
On my bewildered mind;
O let me suffer and not sin,
Be tortured yet resigned.

Through all this world of blinding mist
Still let me look to Thee,
And give me courage to resist
The Tempter till he flee. . . .

O Thou hast taken my delight
And hope of life away,
And bid me watch the painful night
And wait the weary day.

The hope and the delight were Thine:
I bless Thee for their loan;
I gave Thee while I deemed them mine
Too little thanks I own.

Shall I with joy Thy blessings share
And not endure their loss,
Or hope the martyr's Crown to wear
And cast away the Cross?

—*Anne Brontë, 1820–1849*
from "Last Lines"

"Until the day breaks and the shadows flee
away, I will get me to the mountain of myrrh
and to the hill of frankincense."—this has been
Your word, Lord, to me today, with a meaning
hitherto unseen; that the gathering of the bitter-
sweet myrrh of heart-brokenness over failure
and shortcomings, over all the might-have-
beens of the past, can bring us nearer to You
than all the gathering of frankincense on the
hills. Such is Your abounding grace that, even
where sin has abounded, the place where we
wash Your feet with our tears has a great near-
ness to Your holy place above.

—*Lilias Trotter, 1853–1928*
in *Until the Day Breaks: The Life and Work of Lilias Trotter, Pioneer Missionary to Muslim North Africa*, by Patricia St. John, adapted

ॐ

Against self-pity, Man of sorrows, defend me,
With Thy deep sweetness and Thy gentle
power.

—*Violet Alleyn Storey, 20th century*
from "Prayer in Affliction"

Ah! Blissful Lord, why wouldst Thou become Man, and suffer so much pain for my sins, and for all men's sins, that shall be saved; and we so unkind, O Lord, to Thee; and I, most unworthy, cannot suffer this little pain. Ah! Lord, because of Thy great pain, have mercy on my little pain.

For the great pain that Thou suffered, give me not so much as I am worthy, for I may not bear as much as I am worthy. And if Thou wilt, Lord, that I bear it, send me patience.

—*Margery Kempe, c.1373–c.1438*
The Book of Margery Kempe

❧

O Lord, what would you have me do further in this world? I neither see nor hear, nor eat nor sleep. I do not know what I do or what I say. I feel as though I were a dead thing. There is no creature that understands me. I find myself lonely, unknown, poor, naked, strange and different from the rest of the world.

—*Catherine of Genoa, 1447–1510*

Lord, help us to see in your crucifixion and resurrection an example of how to endure and seemingly to die in the agony and conflict of daily life, so that we may live more fully and creatively. . . . Help us to accept the pains and conflicts that come to us each day as opportunities to grow as people and become more like you. Enable us to go through them patiently and bravely, trusting that you will support us.

—*Mother Teresa of Calcutta, 1910–1997*
A Gift for God

❧

A prayer for a couple whose daughter-in-law lay near death:

Dear Heavenly Father, thank You for Your comforting promises. Please be with each one there in that waiting room and in intensive care. Hold the hand of each one right now. You have said You write the name of each believer in the Lamb's Book of Life. We thank You for the Messiah, the Lamb of God, who died to have a victory over death itself. We thank You that Jesus wept at the tomb of Lazarus and that He said that the last enemy that will be destroyed is death itself. Please give the needed grace sufficient for now to that dear couple as they are alone and Your strength in their weakness for the need of now.

—*Edith Schaeffer, 20th century*
The Life of Prayer

O my God! if thou art pleased to render me a spectacle to men and angels, thy holy will be done! All that I ask is, that thou wilt be with and save those who love thee;—so that neither life nor death, neither principalities nor powers, may ever separate them from the love of God which is in Jesus Christ. As for me, what matters it what men think of me, or what they make me suffer, since they cannot separate me from that Saviour? . . . If I can only be accepted of Him, I am willing that all men should despise and hate me. Their strokes will polish what may be defective in me, so that I may be presented in peace to Him, for whom I die daily. . . . O Saviour! I present myself before thee an offering, a sacrifice. Purify me in thy blood.

—*Madame Jeanne Guyon, 1648–1717*
words prayed during her years in the Bastille in *The Autobiography of Madame Guyon*

O Lord, this moment send Your heavenly cameras to take pictures of this cruelty. Hurry, please!

—*Ahn Ei Sook, 20th century*
If I Perish

❧

O Jesus, amiable king and most desirable friend, remember the sorrow Thou hadst, when Thou didst hang naked and wretched on the Cross. . . . I beseech Thee, merciful Jesus, by the sword of grief which then pierced Thy soul, have compassion on me in all my tribulations and afflictions, bodily and spiritual, and give me comfort at the hour of my death.

—*Bridget of Sweden, 1303–1373*
in *St. Bridget of Sweden* by Johannes Jorgensen, translated by Ingeborg Lund

❧

Since grief is my assignment for today, Lord, help me to grieve wholeheartedly, allowing the reality of the grief to possess me until it becomes appropriate to move beyond it.

—*Elizabeth Rooney, 20th century*
in *Bright Legacy: Portraits of Ten Outstanding Christian Women*, edited by Anne Spangler

❧

O Jesus, in that garden where Thou didst see the last night of Thy life descend upon men, and a still darker night upon Thine own soul, Thou didst suffer alone. Even those who loved Thee failed in that critical hour to understand Thee and Thy torture. . . . Remember, then, adored Master, what that hour was to Thee; have pity on our weakness, and do Thou, who art the only Consoler, the only Heart that can share and understand, come and appease and strengthen us, and help us to make our grief a work of salvation and of love, a living preaching of the Gospel.

—*Elisabeth Leseur, 1866–1914*
My Spirit Rejoices

My darling firstborn child thou hast pleased to take from me; and as thy wisdom saw fit not to accept him as servant, I thank thee that thou art pleased to accept him as a saint, spotless and innocent as I received him from thee. Oh that he may be as acceptable an offering as Abraham's only son in thy sight!

—Margaret Hill Morris, 18th century
adapted

è

God, I confess my rage for the times I called to you and heard nothing, for the times I needed you and found you absent, for the times I desperately longed for your comforting embrace and felt only emptiness and abandonment. I have felt forsaken, God, forsaken in my mourning . . . left with only my tears. If only you had heard me, if only you had been present with me . . . .

Out of the depths, God, I cry to you. . . .

I believe, God. . . . I believe that you count my tears. . . . that you are the resurrection and the life.

So I live! I live!

—Kathy Manis Findley, 20th century
Voices of Our Sisters

è

Surrendering

We approach God to give ourselves to him and to ask him for the faith and the resolve to make such a gift.

May my life be a continual prayer, a long act of *love. May nothing* distract me from You, neither noise nor diversions. O my Master, I would so love to live with You in silence. But what I love above all is to do Your will, and since You want me to still remain in the world, I submit with all my heart *for love of You.*

—*Elizabeth Catez, 1880–1906*
Elizabeth of the Trinity: The Complete Works, translated by Sister Aletheia Kane

ॐ

May we let go our all to You as utterly as did the lad with his poor store of loaves and fishes. "All" may mean the last ounce of strength, the last sum of our balance, the last available hour for prayer, but that is the kind of giving we shall long to lay in Your pierced hands when we see You over there. It will be too late for earthly possibilities; it is not too late now, and we do not know what bit of inadequate offering You may use still, as You did then, for the fulcrum of Your power.

—*Lilias Trotter, 1853–1928*
in *Until the Day Breaks: The Life and Work of Lilias Trotter, Pioneer Missionary to Muslim North Africa,* by Patricia St. John, adapted

ॐ

Lord, I want to do your will, even when I don't want to—especially when I don't want to. Have mercy on me. Help me to love you by following your commandments.

—*Priscilla Heidebrecht, 20th century*

ॐ

O Thou to whom, without reserve,
My all I would resign,
I ask for grace and faith to say,
"Thy will, O Lord, not mine!"
In joy or grief, in bliss or pain,
This prayer shall rise to Thee,
"Thy will, not mine, O blessed Lord,
Thy will be done in me!"

—*Fanny Crosby, 1820–1918*
from "Thy Will Be Done in Me"

❧

Teach me to trust your plan, precious Lord, while you prune, trim and direct. Make rest and surrender my habitual life-style.

—*Berit Kjos, 20th century*

❧

O Lord, if you really are the Good Shepherd, then you shall be my shepherd.

—*Eva von Tiele-Winckler, 1866–1930*
in *Women Who Changed the Heart of the City*, by Delores T. Burger

❧

Be thou all in all to us; and may all things earthly, while we bend them to our growth in grace, dwell lightly in our hearts, so that we may readily, or even joyfully, give whatever thou dost ask for.

—*Mary Carpenter, 1807–1877*

❧

What shall I give to him for all his blessing? I can only give my own self—all I have, and all I am. I desire to surrender myself wholly to you, O my God, to live more simply as one set apart for you, not finding my joy and comfort in the earthly blessings you so richly give me, but, while thankful for the gracious gifts, looking only to the Giver as the Source of my happiness and the Object of my life. I cannot shake off the habits of thought and feeling which many years have formed in me; I can only ask you to have mercy on me, poor and needy as I am, and control in me all that is obstinate and sinful. Fill me with your pure and heavenly love, so that all my narrowness and selfishness may be lost in the wideness of your love.

—*Maria Hare, 1807–1870*
adapted

ૐ

O Lord, who call your own sheep by name, grant, we beg you, that all whom you call by the voice of conscience may straightway arise to do your most compassionate will, or abide patiently to suffer it. Amen.

—*Christina Rossetti, 1830–1894*

ૐ

Govern all by your wisdom, O Lord, so that my soul may always be serving you as you will, and not as I may choose. Do not punish me, I beg you, by granting what I wish or ask, if it offends your love which should always live in me. Let me die to myself, that so I may serve you: let me live for you, who . . . are the true life.

—*Teresa of Avila, 1515–1582*

ૐ

O Lord, if this I am now going through is the right road home, then I will not murmur!

—*Rosalind Goforth, 1864–1942*

ૐ

O Wind of God, come bend us, break us,
Till humbly we confess our need.

—Bessie P. Head, 1850–1936
from "O Breath of Life, Come Sweeping through Us"

❧

Your wind breathes where it wishes,
moves where it wills, sometimes
severs my safe moorings. Sovereign gusts—
buffet my winds with your blowing,
loosen me, lift me to go
wherever you're going.

—Luci Shaw, 20th century
from "Pneuma," Polishing the Petoskey Stone

❧

Lord, all I am and hope to be,
I humbly offer, King, to thee!

—Eloise Alberta Veronica Bibb, 1878–1927
from "An Offering"

❧

Yes, Lord, I accept it; I submit, I yield, I pledge
myself to walk in that path, and to follow that
Voice, and to trust Thee with the consequences.

—Catherine Booth, 1829–1890

❧

O my God! Imprint it on my soul with the
strength of the Holy Spirit that, by his grace
supported and defended, I may never more
forget that thou art my all, and that I cannot
be received in thy heavenly kingdom without a
pure and faithful heart supremely devoted to
thy holy will. Oh, keep me for the sake of Jesus
Christ!

—Elizabeth Seton, 1774–1821

❧

Accept me, Lord, as I am and make me such
as thou wouldst have me to be.

—Mary Livingstone, 19th century

God's will be done, and I do humbly thank him that he thinketh me worthy to suffer any kind of death for so good a cause.

—*Margaret Clitherow, c.1556–1586*
words she prayed when being condemned to death for sheltering Catholic priests in her home

❧

Your love, Jesus, is an ocean with no shore to bound it. And if I plunge into it, I carry with me all the possessions I have. You know, Lord, what these possessions are—the souls you have seen fit to link with mine.

—*Thérèse of Lisieux, 1873–1897*

❧

I am the Lord's! Yes; body, soul, and
  spirit . . .
As Thou, Beloved . . .
Forever and forevermore art mine.

—*Lucy A. Bennett, 1850–1927*

Father, thank You for revealing the depth of Your love for me and for not leaving me even though I have resisted You for so long. I now give up my right to my own will. I want to do Your will and be used by You. I will trust You with whatever the future holds. If you want me to work in a foreign country, I will. If You want me to speak in public, although it seems quite impossible, I will. And if You want me to be single in Your service, I will be. I will never seek a marriage partner. If You want me to marry, I will trust You to bring somebody to me. I give You all rights to myself.

—*Pamela Rosewell Moore, 20th century*
Safer Than a Known Way

❧

Thy wonderful grand will, my God!
Triumphantly I make it mine;
And faith shall breathe her glad "Amen"
To every dear command of Thine.

—*Jean Sophia Pigott, 1845–1882*

Speak, Lord, for Thy servant heareth.
Grant us ears to hear,
Eyes to see,
Wills to obey,
Hearts to love;
Then declare what Thou wilt,
Reveal what Thou wilt,
Command what Thou wilt,
Demand what Thou wilt.

—*Christina Rossetti, 1830–1894*

❧

Revive the world, O Lord, beginning with me!

—*Corrie ten Boom, 1893–1983*
Amazing Love

❧

I desire neither the world nor anything that is worldly, and nothing seems to give me pleasure unless it comes from Thee: everything else seems to me a heavy cross. I may well be mistaken and it may be that I have not the desire that I have described; but Thou seest, my Lord, that, so far as I can understand, I am not lying. . . . I know well how little my strength and insufficiency of virtue can achieve if Thou be not ever granting me Thy grace and helping me not to forsake Thee.

—*Teresa of Avila, 1515–1582*
in *The Life of Teresa of Avila*, translated by E. Allison Peers

❧

My life, my all, Lord, I entreat
Take, and use, and make replete
With the love and patience sweet
That made *your* life so complete.

—*Mary Slessor, 1848–1915*

❧

Lord, you have made me the way I am. I love a home, I love security, I love children, and I love him. Yet I feel that marriage under these conditions would draw me away from you. I surrender even this, Lord, and leave it in your hands. Lead me, Lord, and strengthen me. You have promised to fulfill all my needs. I trust in you alone.

—*Henrietta Mears, 1890–1963*
Dream Big

❧

Lord, I make you a present of myself. I do not know what to do with myself. So let me make this exchange: I will place myself entirely in your hands, if you will cover my ugliness with your beauty, and tame my unruliness with your love.

—*Catherine of Genoa, 1447–1510*
in *The HarperCollins Book of Prayers*, compiled by Robert Van de Weyer

Fill with thy Spirit till all shall see
Christ only, always, living in me!

—*Adelaide A. Pollard, 1862–1934*
from "Have Thine Own Way, Lord!"

❧

Lord, I am yours, yours wholly, and yours forever! I am yours by the purchase of your blood, and I present myself to you now as a living sacrifice, body, soul, and spirit to be as clay in your hands.

I give you my heart, Lord, to love only what you love; to hate what you hate; to endure all things, to suffer long and be kind, to be not easily provoked; to think no evil, not to seek my own. Help me, oh my God!

—*Hannah Whitall Smith, 1832–1911*
The Christian's Secret of a Holy Life, edited by Melvin E. Dieter

❧

Speaking Honestly

God invites us to come to him, no matter what we have to say. He desires to be closer than our closest loved one, and he places no restrictions on our honesty before him.

The only way I know to keep up communication right now is to give You a running commentary on how I feel, and it isn't going to be pretty!

—*Marilyn McCord Adams, 20th century*
in *God and the Philosophers*, edited by Thomas V. Morris

❧

Well, God, I'm here.

—*mother of two small children, 20th century*
praying for the first time in years

❧

From silly devotions
and from sour-faced saints,
good Lord, deliver us.

—*Teresa of Avila, 1515–1582*

❧

O God, you know how much I am distressed, for I have told you again and again. Now, God, help me. . . . If you were in trouble, as I am, and I could help you, as you can me, think I wouldn't do it? Yes, God, you *know* I would do it. O God, you know I have no money, but you can make the people do for me, and you must make the people do for me. I will never give you peace till you do, God. O God, make the people hear me—don't let them turn me off, without hearing and helping me.

—*Sojourner Truth, c.1797–1883*

❧

"Let the words of my mouth, and the meditation of my heart, be acceptable in thy sight, O Lord, my strength, and my redeemer."

If it were just a matter of the mouth,
I wouldn't have so much trouble,

but it isn't,

and I do.

—*Lois A. Cheney, 20th century*
God Is No Fool

❧

Lord, is all well? Oh, tell me. . . .
Do *Thou* speak; is all well?

—*Amy Carmichael, 1867–1951*
Rose From Brier

❧

O Lord God! I trusted in you;
O my beloved Jesus! Free me now;
In callous chains, in penalty's pains,
I long for you.
Fainting, searching and genuflecting
I adore you and implore you to free me.

—*Mary, Queen of Scots, 1542–1587*

❧

Love Letter

I hate you, God.
Love, Madeleine.

I write my message on water
and at bedtime I tiptoe upstairs
and let it flow under your door.

When I am angry with you
I know that you are there
even if you do not answer my knock
even when your butler opens the door an inch
and flaps his thousand wings in annoyance
at such untoward interruption
and says the master is not at home.

I love you, Madeleine,
Hate, God.

(This is how I treat my friends, he said to
   one great saint.
No wonder you have so few, Lord, she replied.)

I cannot turn the other cheek
it takes all the strength I have
to keep from hitting back

the soldiers bayonet the baby
the little boys trample the old woman

the gutters are filled with groans
while pleasure-seekers knock each other down
to get their tickets stamped first.

I'm turning in my ticket
and my letter of introduction
you're supposed to do the knocking.

How can I write to you
to tell you that I'm angry
when I've been given the wrong address
and I don't even know your right name?

I take hammer and nails
and tack my message on two crossed pieces
   of wood.

Dear God,
is it too much to ask you
to bother to be?
Just show your hindquarters
and let me hear you roar.

Love,
Madeleine.

—*Madeleine L'Engle, 20th century*
The Irrational Season

106

Lord Jesus, You want honest words on my lips; no thought of mine is hidden from You anyway . . . I am puzzled about the Father's timing. . . . Lord, why does Your providence have to move so slowly? I know that the seasons come and go in majestic rhythm. No prayers of mine could change any of this. I know that Your ways are not my ways; Your timing is not my timing. But Lord, how do I, so earthbound, come to terms with the pace of eternity?

—*Catherine Marshall, 1915–1983*
Adventures in Prayer

❧

Save me from leading an imaginary life in the ideas of others, and so to be eager and forward in showing myself to the world. Forbid that I should retain, improve and adorn this fictitious being, while stupidly neglecting the truth. Help me not to contend with men's interests, prejudices, and passions, that rarely admit of a calm dispute, when it can innocently be avoided. May I be so far a lover of myself as to prefer the peace and tranquility of my own mind before that of others, and if, after doing all that I can to make others happy, they yet remain obstinately bent to follow those ways that lead to misery, I leave them to your mercy.

—*Susanna Wesley, 1669–1742*

❧

Please help me to be real, to say things . . . in music or in my gardening, painting, building . . . true to what I am honestly and sincerely communicating of repentance, of asking for mercy, of bringing praise or thanksgiving, or making as a tribute to You, Heavenly Father, for the enjoyment Your creation has given to me.

—*Edith Schaeffer, 20th century*
The Life of Prayer

❧

After realizing that her name should be Sojourner *because of her calling to "travel up and down the land, showing the people their sins, and being a sign unto them," she prayed:*

Oh, God, give me a name with a *handle* to it. *Sojourner Truth*

Why, thank you, God. That is a good name. Thou art my last Master, and thy name is Truth; and Truth shall be my abiding name till I die!

—*Sojourner Truth, c. 1799–1883*

৯

Lord, I want to please You. I want to serve You. I want to use what You have given me to help others. But I can't seem to do it. I can't keep up the pace. I feel torn and frustrated and exhausted. I'm trying to please *everybody,* and I'm pleasing no one. I'm trying to do everything, and I seem to accomplish nothing.

—*Lynne Hybels, 20th century*
The Joy of Personal Worship

Lord, I can't think of anything else to say.

—*Eugenia Price, 20th century*
Early Will I Seek Thee

৯

Words prayed in response to the Biblical story of Hannah in I Samuel 1–2:11

I won't just move my lips in a song or in a prayer: God make me true, like Hannah. I won't take offense when someone says something to me which I don't like; God make me humble-hearted, like Hannah. And when Thou dost ask me to give up something to Thee, by Thy grace I will sing and rejoice, like Hannah.

—*Amy Carmichael, 1867–1951*
Whispers of His Power

৯

What profit is there in my death? . . . Will the dust praise Thee? There will be one soul less in this world to serve and praise You and, by the way, there aren't too many of us left.

—*Corrie ten Boom, 1893–1983*
words prayed during World War II in *Return to the Hiding Place*

❧

God, I don't have any friends. . . . You're going to have to be my friend, my best friend.

—*Sonja Carson, 20th century*
in *Think Big,* by Benjamin Carson

❧

I hadn't really thought of inviting you in, Lord. I sort of thought I'd just keep handing you bits and pieces of my life, like feeding a tramp at the back door without letting him in to mess up the kitchen. You know and I know that I need to let you in. So here goes everything. . . .

—*Elizabeth Rooney, 20th century*

❧

Lord, I believe, because I want to believe.

—*Dorothy Day, 1897–1980*

❧

You whose birth broke all the
social & biological rules—
son of the poor who accepted
the worship due a king—
child prodigy debating with
the Temple Th.D.s—you
were the kind who used
a new math
to multiply bread, fish, faith.
You practiced a
radical sociology:
rehabilitated con men &
call girls. You valued women
& other minority groups.
A G.P., you specialized in
heart transplants.
Creator, healer,
shepherd, innovator,
story-teller, weather-maker,
botanist, alchemist,
exorcist, iconoclast,
seeker, seer, motive-sifter,

you were always beyond,
above us. Ahead
of your time, & ours.

And we would like
to be *like* you. Bold
as Boanerges, we hear ourselves
demand: "Admit us
to your avant-garde.
Grant us degree
in all the liberal arts
of heaven."
Why our belligerence?
Why does this whiff of fame
and greatness smell so sweet?
Why must we compete
to be first? Have we forgotten
how you took, simply, cool water
and a towel for our feet?

—*Luci Shaw, 20th century*
"He who would be great among you," *Polishing the Petoskey Stone*

Father, like Thomas we confess our doubts to you, our struggles of faith. We thank you for your gracious understanding of, and yes, even your provision for, these doubts. Your complete acceptance of us and your complete knowledge of us allow us to put aside pretense, to drop our facade. Our tomorrows and our yesterdays are mercifully covered by your gracious love. We trust your finished work.

—*April Carlson, 20th century*

❧

God, if there be a God, if you will prove to me that you are, and if you will give me peace, I will give you my whole life. I'll do anything you ask me to do, go where you send me, obey you all my days.

—*Isobel Kuhn, 1901–1957*

❧

Lord, I've had it! I've had it up to here. I just can't take any more. I feel like going away, running off and hiding. . . .
Go ahead.
I beg Your pardon, Lord?
Go ahead and hide. Hide . . . in Me.

—*Carole Mayhall, 20th century*
From the Heart of a Woman

❧

Lord, lead me away from my tendency to blame others for my problems. Give me a friend who knows more about grace than I do. Grant me the humility to open up honestly to you and another person about the hidden struggles of my heart.

—*Rose Marie Miller, 20th century*
From Fear to Freedom

❧

111

O Eternal Father! Forgive my ignorance, that I presume thus to chatter to You, but the love of Your Mercy will be my excuse before the Face of Your loving-kindness.

—*Catherine of Siena, 1347–1380*
The Dialogue, translated by Algar Thorold

≈

Lord, if being a martyr for thee would glorify thee, all right; just to go down there and be butchered by wicked men for their own gratification, without any reference to thy glory, I'm not willing.

—*Amanda Smith, 1837–1915*

≈

Prayer of a single mom

Rough day today, Lord. I hate the *trapped* feeling of single parenting. I am so depressed and confused. Even after seven years, I still carry pain and loneliness inside as constant companions.

I'm tired of trying to keep up with everything. Tired of trying to build a framework and having it collapse around me. Tired of women who work part-time, and have sitters, housekeepers, and husbands who make good salaries—they tell *me* not to be so serious and stressed out! "Why don't you take up running and spend more time with your son?"

I know I must take charge of my life, and I am doing the best I can. But, Lord, I honestly don't know how to do anything differently. I can't fake having a better life, and I can't find it either. And my Christian friends with easy answers aren't helping—they can't even understand.

It hurts so badly to be so disconnected from myself and others. Where do I go from here, God?

—*Dreama Plybon Love, 20th century*

≈

Grant us grace, Almighty Father,
So to pray as to deserve to be heard.

—Jane Austen, 1775–1817

&

Here I am, Lord, send me, even horrible un-loving me, if that is what you want to do. And I will trust you to do whatever you want and to make me willing and able to let you have your way in my life, even though this looks to be the most preposterous, presumptuous, and absurd thing that you have yet led me to do.

—Hannah Hurnard, 1905–1990
words prayed after realizing God wanted her to go to Israel as a missionary during the 1940s, in *Thou Shalt Remember*

&

Words offered by a Chinese woman as a group of Christians were meeting in her home to pray, even though they had no leader, no Bibles, and no hymnals. (The Sunday after this prayer, God gave her the gift of preaching.)

God, this kind of situation should not be! You must send a servant to us. And if you don't send a servant, next Sunday I'm going to lock the door and not let anyone in. We will stop! I am not educated, so how do You expect me to manage? And we have no one to sing hymns of praise. What do You expect me to do? You must send Your servant.

—Unnamed Chinese woman in the village of Lincun, 20th century
in *Wise as Serpents Harmless as Doves: Christians in China Tell Their Story*, edited by Jonathan Chao and Richard Van Houten

&

Expressing Love

When we stop to recognize God's immense, incomparable love for us, we may at first be speechless. Then, we glimpse the astounding truth that though God understands our silent awe, yet he joys in our responses, our *expressions* of love.

I love thee. Thus far I can speak, but all the rest is unutterable; and I must leave the pleasing tale untold, until I can talk in the language of immortality; and then I'll begin the transporting story, which shall never come to an end, but be still and still beginning; for thy beauties, O thou fairest of ten thousand! will still be new, and shall kindle fresh ardor in my soul to all eternity.

—*Elizabeth Singer Rowe, 1674–1737*
Devout Exercises of the Heart

❧

O immeasurably tender love! Who would not be set afire with such love? What heart could keep from breaking? You, deep well of charity, it seems you are so madly in love with your creatures that you could not live without us! Yet you are our God, and have no need of us. . . . What could move you to such mercy? Neither duty nor any need you have of us (we are sinful and wicked debtors!)—but only love!

—*Catherine of Siena, 1347–1380*
The Dialogue, translated by Suzanne Noffke

❧

Father, I cringe to see that I have been believing a lie: That since I have tried to serve You, I have a right to ask for Your blessings.

Now I understand, Father, that You must manifest love and joy to us, Your creatures, because You are love and joy; that You, as the Sun of Righteousness in whom no darkness dwells, shine upon us because it is Your nature to shine—not because a one of us is deserving of it.

—*Catherine Marshall, 20th century*
Adventures in Prayer, adapted

 za

Teach us, O Lord, to fear you without being afraid; to fear you in love that we may love you without fear.

—*Christina Rossetti, 1830–1894*

za

Your love is like a white dove with orange flames bursting from its wings. The dove brings the promise of peace to my troubled soul, and the flames promise joy to my miserable heart.

—*Hildegard of Bingen, 1098–1179*
in *The HarperCollins Book of Prayers,* compiled by Robert Van de Weyer

za

. . . O take Thine own,
. . . Thy love's own flowers,
. . . to make Thy crown.

—*Amy Carmichael, 1867–1951*
Rose from Brier

za

God, my God . . . what I know very definitely is that your love is my only treasure. . . . For if I have other joys . . . I know very well that if one day you definitely made it known to me that your love had never dwelt in my Soul, all joy would be extinguished for me and I should have lost my reason for living.

—Raissa Maritain, 1883–1960
Raissa's Journal, presented by Jacques Maritain

❧

God of the sky,
God of the sea,
God of the rock
and bird and tree,
you are also
the God of me.

The pebble fell.
The water stirred
and stilled again.
The hidden bird
made song for you.
His praise you heard.

You heard him sing
from in the tree.
And searching still
I know you'll see
the love that wings
to you from me.

—Luci Shaw, 20th century
"Small song," *Polishing the Petoskey Stone*

❧

Lord of Glory, who hast bought us
With Thy life-blood as the price,
Never grudging for the lost ones
That tremendous sacrifice,
Give us faith to trust Thee boldly,
Hope, to stay our souls on Thee;
But, oh! best of all Thy graces,
Give us Thine own charity.

—*Eliza S. Alderson, 1818–1889*
from "Lord of Glory, Who Hast Bought Us"

&

You loved me, without my having loved You.
Oh, Fire of Love! Thanks, thanks be to You,
Eternal Father! I am imperfect and full of darkness, and You, Perfection and Light, have
shown to me perfection. . . . I was dead, and
You have brought me to life.

—*Catherine of Siena, 1347–1380*
The Dialogue, translated by Algar Thorold

&

Almighty God, I can love all, but the only one
I will love in particular is you, only you.

—*Mother Teresa of Calcutta, 1910–1997*
The Mother Teresa Reader

&

Prayer of love for a new baby

O God, you are love itself, and you have shed
light and love into my soul. Only you know
how the seams of my heart are bursting with
affection for this little mite.

—*Helen Good Brenneman, 20th century*
Meditations for the New Mother

&

I care now about one thing only—to love You, my Jesus! Great deeds are forbidden me, I cannot preach the Gospel nor shed my blood—but what does it matter? . . . Love proves itself by deeds, so how am I to show my love? Well, I will scatter flowers, perfuming the divine Throne with their fragrance, and I'll sweetly sing my hymn of love. . . . These flowers are every little sacrifice, every glance and word, and the doing of the least of actions for love. . . . Thus will I scatter my flowers. I will never find one without plucking its petals for You and I shall sing, sing without ceasing even if I have to gather my roses from the midst of thorns.

—*Thérèse of Lisieux, 1873–1897*
The Autobiography of St. Thérèse of Lisieux, translated by John Beevers

❧

Father in heaven, thank you that you do not leave us comfortless. You come to us, enveloping us in your complete love even as you ask us to look closely at what is dark within us. And in this way you enable us to break the bonds of sin and the patterns of generations. Thank you for your deep, deep, unqualified love.

—*April Carlson, 20th century*

❧

More love to Thee, O Christ,
More love to Thee!
Hear Thou the prayer I make
On bended knee;
This is my earnest plea:

More love, O Christ, to Thee,
More love to Thee,
More love to Thee.

—*Elizabeth P. Prentiss, 1818–1878*
from "More Love to Thee, O Christ"

❧

I know some beautiful—in you, Lord—thin people. I know some beautiful—in you, Lord—round people. And I can't see that you prefer one above the other, but you love both kinds infinitely. . . .

I'm ready to stop looking at the size of my exterior and start examining my heart. Do I have enough capacity of heart to receive all the blessings you want to give me? And to impart them to others? If I don't, Lord, enlarge my heart. That's so important, you can forget about shrinking my outside.

—*Irene Burk Harrell, 20th century*
Multiplied by Love

Dear Lord,

You are truly the Lover of my soul. Thank you for wooing me at the very times when I am most unlovable. Thank you for forgiving all my unfaithfulness. How can I run after other gods—gods who do not satisfy, gods who rob and enslave me? I thank you that there is no use trying to hide myself from you. It is such a relief to cast off pretense!

Thank you for giving me the beautiful clothes of Jesus Christ and his righteousness. Thank you that you will never disappoint me—that all my longings will be met in you, come what may. Even if I must suffer, I know that you will work all things for my good.

Thank you for being the God of all hope and for filling me with such joy, peace, and gratitude that I am overflowing in a way I never thought possible. Help me to hold fast to you and to serve you with all my heart and soul. Keep me close to your side, and cover me with your wings. Amen.

—*Elsa L. Stewart, 20th century*

Yes, Lord, . . . teach me about love, how to receive it and how to give it.

—*Deborah Strubel, 20th century*
Single, Whole & Holy

Jesus, thou faithful lover, to take the cross and follow thee, where love and duty lead, shall be my portion and my praise.

—*Madame Jeanne Guyon, 1648–1717*
from "The Joy of the Cross," adapted

&

A prayer to be filled with God's love in order to help a hurting person

Pour into me yourself. Love this being through me. Touch her, using me as an instrument. You alter this disharmony, this dissonance. Incarnate me with your life. Let it spring from me to this body of pain. Amen.

—*Karen Burton Mains, 20th century*
Karen! Karen!

&

I do not want that which proceedeth from Thee; I want Thyself alone, O tender Love.

—*Catherine of Genoa, 1447–1510*
in The Mystical Element of Religion as Studied in Saint Catherine of Genoa and Her Friends by Baron Friedrich von Hugel

&

O how magnificent is the compassion of the Saving One.

—*Hildegard of Bingen, 1098–1179*
Hildegard of Bingen's Book of Divine Works with Letters and Songs, edited by Matthew Fox

&

Singing Out Thanks and Praise

With so many reasons to thank and praise our God, it is a good thing we have all eternity to sing!

Lord, the angels delight
in praising you,
They fill the heavens
with their perfect songs,
serenading you with eternal love.
I, too, desire to worship you.
Please accept the melody
of gratitude—the faint echo
of the angelic chorus—that springs
from my own heart.

—*Anna Trimiew, 20th century*

❧

All praise to Him who now hath turned
My fears to joys, my sighs to song,
My tears to smiles, my sad to glad.

—*Anne Bradstreet, 1612–1672*

❧

Through Thy grace alone I have been enabled
to give myself wholly and forever to Thee.
Thou hast given Thy Word, assuring me that
Thou dost receive. I believe that Word! Alleluia!
The Lord God Omnipotent reigneth unrivaled
in my heart. Glory be to the Father! Glory be
to the Son! Glory be to the Holy Spirit forever!

—*Phoebe Palmer, 19th century*
in *Fragrant Memories of the Tuesday Meeting*

❧

Part of a running conversation with God upon entering church

I bow before You. You're here! You've been with me all along—praise You for that—but it's special to meet You here together with the Body.

What part of Yourself will You show today, Lord? You're exciting. Sometimes You show us Your tenderness, Your "still, small voice"— sometimes You thunder. You know my need. I'm ready.

O great God of the heavens! You are matchless. . . . You are worthy. You are glorious.

—*Anne Ortlund, 20th century*
Up with Worship

ঽ

We bring no glittering treasures,
No gems from earth's deep mine;
We come, with simple measures,
To chant Thy love divine.
Children, thy favors sharing,
Their voice of thanks would raise;

Father, accept our offering,
Our song of grateful praise. . . .

Redeemer, grant thy blessing!
O teach us how to pray,
That each, thy fear possessing,
May tread life's onward way;
Then, where the pure are dwelling
We hope to meet again,
And, sweeter numbers swelling,
Forever praise thy name.

—*Harriett C. Phillips, 1806–1884*
from "We Bring No Glittering Treasures"

ঽ

Sing to the Lord, for he has triumphed gloriously.

—*Miriam of the Bible*
Exodus 15:21a, *New Revised Standard Version of the Bible*

ঽ

Oooh, my good and holy Father, what can I say to Thee for Thy blessings?

—*Sister Kelly, 19th century*
words prayed at age twelve on the occasion of her conversion, in *Can I Get a Witness? Prophetic Religious Voices of African American Women*, edited by Marcia Y. Riggs

🙐

You have made me so rich, O God, please let me share out Your beauty with open hands. My life has become an uninterrupted dialogue with You, O God, one great dialogue. Sometimes when I stand in some corner of the camp, my feet planted on Your earth, my eyes raised towards Your Heaven, tears . . . run down my face, tears of deep emotion and gratitude. At night, too, when I lie in my bed and rest in You, O God, tears of gratitude run down my face, and that is my prayer.

—*Etty Hillesum, d. 1943*
diary entry set in Westerbork transit camp in Holland, where she volunteered to go, accompanying the first group of Jews to be randomly swept up in Amsterdam by the Nazis

O the wonderful power of God that I have seen, and the experiences that I have had! . . . God's power is as great now, and as sufficient to save, as when he preserved Daniel in the Lions Den, or the three Children in the Fiery Furnace. I may well say . . . "O give thanks unto the Lord, for he is good, for his mercy endureth for ever. Let the Redeemed of the Lord say so, whom he hath redeemed from the hand of the Enemy."

—*Mary Rowlandson, c. 1637–1711*
A True History of the Captivity and Restoration of Mrs. Mary Rowlandson, written after her release from nearly twelve weeks as a captive of the Narragansett Indians

🙐

My God, I thank Thee who hast made
The earth so bright;
So full of splendor and of joy,
Beauty and light;
So many glorious things are here,
Noble and right!

I thank Thee, too, that Thou hast made
Joy to abound;
So many gentle thoughts and deeds
Circling us round,
That in the darkest spot of earth
Some love is found.

I thank Thee more that all our joy
Is touched with pain;
That shadows fall on brightest hours;
That thorns remain;
So that earth's bliss may be our guide,
And not our chain.

—*Adelaide Anne Procter, 1825–1864*
from "Thankfulness"

❧

Blessed be God
for all, all, all.

—*Alla Renee Bozarth, 20th century*
in *Earth Prayers from Around the World,* by Elizabeth Roberts and
Elias Amidon

❧

How wonderful, O my God . . . has been thy
protection over me! How many perils have I
passed through in going over mountains, and
on the edges of steep and terrible cliffs! . . .
How often have I been exposed to be thrown
headlong from frightful heights into hideous
torrents. . . . Thou, O God, didst guard me in
such imminent dangers. . . . In thee my soul
trusted.

—*Madame Jeanne Guyon, 1648–1717*
in *Life, Religious Opinions and Experience of Madame Guyon,* by
Thomas C. Upham

❧

all the field praises Him/all
dandelions are His glory/gold
and silver/all trilliums unfold
white flames above their trinities
of leaves all wild strawberries
and massed wood violets reflect His skies'
clean blue and white
all brambles/all oxeyes
all stalks and stems lift to His light
all young windflower bells
tremble on hair
springs for His air's
carillon touch/last year's yarrow (raising
brittle star skeletons) tells
age is not past praising
all small low unknown
unnamed weeds show His impossible greens
all grasses sing
tone on clear tone
all mosses spread a spring-
soft velvet for His feet
and by all means
all leaves/buds/all flowers cup
jewels of fire and ice

holding up
to His kind morning heat
a silver sacrifice

now
make of our hearts a field
to raise Your praise.

—*Luci Shaw, 20th century*
"May 20: very early morning," *Polishing the Petoskey Stone*

❧

Made for Thyself, O God!
Made for Thy love, Thy service, Thy delight;
Made to show forth Thy wisdom, grace and
    might;
Made for Thy praise, whom veiled
    archangels laud;
O strange and glorious thought, that we
    may be
A joy to Thee.

—*Frances Ridley Havergal, 1836–1879*

❧

Almighty and Eternal God, the Disposer of all the affairs of the world, there is not one circumstance so great as not to be subject to thy power, nor so small but it comes within thy care.

—*Queen Anne, 1665–1714*

❧

Triumphant Saviour, Thee we praise . . .
Thy death is all our gain.

—*Sister M. Cherubim Schaefer, 20th century*
from "Rejoice, Let Alleluias Ring"

❧

The glorious armies of the sky
To thee, Almighty King,
Triumphant anthems consecrate,
And hallelujahs sing.

But still their most exalted flights
Fall vastly short of thee:
How distant then must human praise
From thy perfections be!

Yet how, my God, shall I refrain
When to my ravished sense
Each creature everywhere around
Displays thy excellence! . . .

Thy numerous works exalt thee thus,
And shall I silent be?
No, rather let me cease to breathe,
Than cease from praising thee!

—*Elizabeth Singer Rowe, 1674–1737*
from "Praise"

❧

Because Thy love constraineth, I'll praise Thee evermore!

—*Lucy A. Bennett, 1850–1927*

❧

Begin a song to my God with tambourines,
sing to my Lord with cymbals.
Raise to him a new psalm;
exalt him, and call upon his name.
For the Lord is a God who crushes wars;
he sets up his camp among his people;
he delivered me from the hands of my
   pursuers. . . .
I will sing to my God a new song:
O Lord, you are great and glorious,
wonderful in strength, invincible.
Let all your creatures serve you,
for you spoke, and they were made.
You sent forth your spirit, and it formed
   them;
there is none that can resist your voice.
For the mountains shall be shaken to their
   foundations with the waters;
before your glance the rocks shall melt like
   wax.
But to those who fear you, you show mercy.

—Judith of the Apocrypha
Judith 16:1-2, 13-15, *New Revised Standard Version with the*
Apocryphal/Deuterocanonical Books

We thank thee for those people who plant gardens wherever they are. We thank thee for the vision, the inspiration they give to others and for the legacy of love which they leave for those who come after. Help us, each in our own way to garden as we go.

—Josephine Robertson, 20th century
Meditations on Garden Themes

ॐ

We thank Thee with all our hearts for every gracious dispensation, for all the blessings that have attended our lives, for every hour of safety, health and peace, of domestic comfort and innocent enjoyment. We feel that we have been blessed far beyond anything that we have deserved; and though we cannot but pray for a continuance of all these mercies, we acknowledge our unworthiness of them and implore Thee to pardon the presumption of our desires.

—Jane Austen, 1775–1817

O infinite goodness of my God! . . . O Joy of the angels, how I long . . . to be wholly consumed in love for Thee! . . . Oh, how good a Friend art Thou, my Lord! How Thou dost comfort us and suffer us and wait until our nature becomes more like Thine and meanwhile dost bear with it as it is!

—*Teresa of Avila, 1515–1582*
in *Life of Teresa of Avila*, translated by E. Allison Peers

Hannah of the Bible, who was childless for years and years, offered this prayer of thanksgiving to God after he fulfilled her longing for a child:

My heart rejoices in the Lord;
in the Lord my horn is lifted high.
My mouth boasts over my enemies,
for I delight in your deliverance.

There is no one holy like the Lord;
there is no one besides you;
there is no Rock like our God.
Do not keep talking so proudly

or let your mouth speak such arrogance,
for the Lord is a God who knows,
and by him deeds are weighed.
The bows of the warriors are broken,
but those who stumbled are armed with
    strength.
Those who were full hire themselves out for
    food,
but those who were hungry hunger no more.
She who was barren has borne seven
    children,
but she who has had many sons pines away.

The Lord brings death and makes alive;
he brings down to the grave and raises up.
The Lord sends poverty and wealth;
he humbles and he exalts.
He raises the poor from the dust
and lifts the needy from the ash heap;
he seats them with princes
and has them inherit a throne of honor.

For the foundations of the earth are the
    Lord's;
upon them he has set the world.

He will guard the feet of his saints,
but the wicked will be silenced in darkness.

It is not by strength that one prevails;
those who oppose the Lord will be shattered.
He will thunder against them from heaven;
the Lord will judge the ends of the earth.

He will give strength to his king
and exalt the horn of his anointed.

> —*Hannah*
> 1 Samuel 2:1-10, *New International Version of the Holy Bible*

❧

O King of saints, we give thee praise and
    glory
For the bright cloud of witnesses unseen,
Whose names shine forth like stars, in sacred
    story,
Guiding our steps to realms of light serene.

And for thy hidden saints, our praise
    adoring,
Fount of all sanctity, to thee we yield,
Who in thy treasurehouse on high art storing
Jewels whose luster was, on earth,
    concealed. . . .

> —*Mary A. Thomson, 1834–1923*
> from "O King of Saints, We Give Thee Praise and Glory"

❧

Lord,

Thank you for being the kind of God who has numbered even the hairs on my head. I love to remember that you have journeyed to the springs of the sea and walked in the recesses of the deep. You know when mountain goats give birth! And the eagle soars at your command! You determine the number of stars and call them each by name! How great you are and how worthy!

Help me to meet you many times throughout the day, to praise you, and to worship and adore you. Thank you that your love is perfect and unfailing. You are my portion and my reward! Blessed be your name! Amen.

—*Elsa L. Stewart, 20th century*

❧

O Saviour, precious Saviour,
Whom yet unseen we love,
O Name of might and favor,
All other names above!
We worship Thee, we bless Thee,
To Thee, O Christ, we sing;
We praise Thee, and confess Thee,
Our holy Lord and King.

—*Frances Ridley Havergal, 1836–1879*
from "O Saviour, Precious Saviour"

❧

God, sometimes I marvel that you answer our needs. You know ahead of time that with those answers, the intensity of our cries for You can diminish. Is it that You want to celebrate our reprieve with us? In any case, we thank you.

—*Ruth Richardson, 20th century*

❧

See how the rising sun
Pursues his shining way;
And wide proclaims his Maker's praise,
With every brightening ray.

Thus would my rising soul
Its heavenly parent sing;
And to its great original,
The humble tribute bring.

Serene I laid me down
Beneath his guardian care;
I slept, and I awoke, and found
My kind preserver near!

O how shall I repay
The bounties of my God?
This feeble spirit pants beneath
The pleasing, painful load.

Dear Saviour, to thy cross
I bring my sacrifice;
By thee perfumed it shall ascend
With fragrance to the skies.

My life I would anew
Devote, O Lord, to thee;
And in thy presence I would spend
A long eternity.

—Elizabeth Scott, c.1708–c.1776
"See How the Rising Sun"

&

Great God, accept our gratitude,
  For the great gifts on us bestowed—
For raiment, shelter and for food.

Great God, our gratitude we bring,
  Accept our humble offering,
For all the gifts on us bestowed,
Thy name be evermore adored.

—Josephine Delphine Henderson Heard, 1861–1921
"Doxology"

&

My soul magnifies the Lord,
and my spirit rejoices in God my Savior,
for he has regarded the low estate of his
    handmaiden.
For behold, henceforth all generations will
    call me blessed;
for he who is mighty has done great things
    for me,
and holy is his name.
And his mercy is on those who fear him
from generation to generation.
He has shown strength with his arm,
he has scattered the proud in the
    imagination of their hearts,
he has put down the mighty from their
    thrones,
and exalted those of low degree;
he has filled the hungry with good things,
and the rich he has sent empty away.
He has helped his servant Israel,
in remembrance of his mercy,
as he spoke to our fathers,
to Abraham and to his posterity for ever.

—*The Virgin Mary*
Gospel of Luke 1:46-55, *Revised Standard Version of the Bible*

⁔

O that I had a thousand hearts, a thousand
hands; all should be employed for God, for he
is worthy. Sing, O my soul. . . .

—*Lady Huntington, 1707–1791*
in *Lady Huntington and Her Friends,* adapted

⁔

All that Spring, with bounteous hand,
Scatters o'er the smiling land;
All that liberal Autumn pours
From her rich o'erflowing stores:

These to thee, my God, we owe,—
Source whence all our blessings flow!
And for these my soul shall raise
Grateful vows and solemn praise.

Yet should rising whirlwinds tear
From its stem the ripening ear,
Should the fig-tree's blasted shoot
Drop her green untimely fruit,—

Should the vine put forth no more,
Nor the olive yield her store,—
Though the sickening flocks should fall,
And the herds desert the stall,—

Should thine altered hand restrain
The early and the latter rain,
Blast each opening bud of joy,
And the rising year destroy;—

Yet to thee my soul should raise
Grateful vows and solemn praise,

And, when every blessing's flown,
Love thee—for thyself alone.

—*Anna L. Barbauld, 1743–1825*
from "Praise to God, Immortal Praise"

&

O glorious God, your outstretched arms are my salvation.

—*Pamela Crosby, 20th century*
365 Meditations for Mothers of Teens

&

The whole world is asleep, and God so full of goodness, so great, so worthy of all praise, no one is thinking of Him! See, nature praises Him, and man . . . who ought to praise Him, sleeps! Let us go, let us go and wake up the universe . . . and sing His praises.

—*Mariam Baouardy, 1846–1878*
in *Mariam: The Little Arab* by Amedée Brunot, translated by Jeanne Dumais

Biographical Index

Adams, Marilyn McCord (20th century). Philosopher, author, and Episcopal priest. *104*
Alcott, Louisa May (1832–1888). American author of *Little Women*. *28*
Alderson, Eliza S. (1818–1889). American hymn writer. *119*
Alexander, Margaret Abigail Walker (20th century). American author. *88*
Alford, Janie (20th century). Poet. *74*
Anna Sophia of Hesse-Darmstadt (1638–1683). No information available. *26*
Anne, Queen (1665–1714). Queen of Great Britain and Ireland. *129*
Auber, Harriet (1773–1862). English poet and hymn writer. *60*
Austen, Jane (1775–1817). English novelist. *78, 113, 130*
Aylward, Gladys (1902–1970). English missionary to China. *75*
Banfield, Mary Grace. No information available. *76*
Baouardy, Mariam (1846–1878). Lebanese mystic. *61, 136*
Barbauld, Anna L. (1743–1825). English poet; author of *Hymns in Prose for Children*. *136*
Barnes, Emilie (20th century). Speaker and author of several books, including *If Teacups Could Talk*. *76*
Bennett, Lucy A. (1850–1927). Hymn writer. *100, 129*
Bethune, Mary McLeod (1875–1955). African-American educator and college president. *79*
Bibb, Eloise Alberta Veronica (1878–1927). African-American poet. *99*
Booth, Catherine (1829–1890). English author, evangelist, "Mother" of the Salvation Army, and wife of William Booth. *20, 99*
Bozarth, Alla Renee (20th century). Episcopal priest, poet, and author. *127*
Bradstreet, Anne (1612–1672). English-born colonial poet. *25, 59, 124*
Brand, Evelyn Harris (1879–1974). Missionary to India, "Granny Brand," mother of author and missionary doctor Paul Brand. *88*
Brenneman, Helen Good (20th century). Writer. *29, 119*
Bridges, Madeline (1840–1920). American poet and humorist. *85*
Bridget of Sweden (1303–1373). Visionary and founder of the Brigittines, a Catholic community of both nuns and priests. *48, 93*
Briscoe, Jill (20th century). English-born Bible teacher and writer. *26, 81*
Brontë, Anne (1820–1849). English novelist. *23, 90*
Brooke, Avery (20th century). Writer of books about spiritual life. *42*
Browning, Elizabeth Barrett (1806–1861). English poet. *61, 72*

Calvin, Ida (1505–1549). Wife of John Calvin. *31*

Carberry, Ethna (1866–1902). Irish poet whose poems are collected in *The Four Winds of Erinn*. *52*

Carlson, April (20th century). Wife, mother of three, grandmother of ten, and licensed clinical social worker. *111, 120*

Carmichael, Amy (1867–1951). Irish author, missionary, and founder of the Dohnavur Fellowship for girls in India. *56, 76, 105, 108, 117*

Carpenter, Mary (1807–1877). Missionary to India. *97*

Carson, Sonja (20th century). Mother of physician and *Gifted Hands* author, Ben Carson. *109*

Cassidy, Sheila (20th century). English surgeon, former political prisoner in Chile, and author of *Prayer for Pilgrims* and *Audacity to Believe*. *62*

Catez, Elizabeth (1880–1906). French Carmelite writer. *47, 96*

Catherine of Genoa (1447–1510). Author and wealthy Italian mystic who served the sick and poor. *37, 57, 91, 102, 122*

Catherine of Siena (1347–1380). Dominican nun, known for her letters on many subjects. *16, 40. 48, 81, 112, 116, 119*

Cheney, Lois A. (20th century). Writer and speech professor. *14, 105*

Cherry, Edith G. (1872–1897). Hymn writer. *24*

Christenson, Evelyn (20th century). Founding president of United Prayer Ministries and author of several books, including *What Happens When Women Pray*. *25, 86*

Clarkson, Margaret (20th century). Canadian author, hymn writer, and teacher. *68*

Clitherow, Margaret (c. 1556–1586). English Catholic martyr. *100*

Coates, Florence Earle (1850–1927). American poet. *49*

Coleridge, Mary (1861–1907). English poet and novelist. *58*

Crosby, Fanny (1820–1918). Poet and hymn writer. *97*

Crosby, Pamela (20th century). Account executive and freelance writer. *136*

Cutts, Mary (1801–1882). Vermont native, biographer, and poet. *55*

Davies, Mary Carolyn (20th century). American poet. *75*

Day, Dorothy (1897–1980). American journalist and reformer. *109*

de Armida, Concepción Cabrera (1862–1937). Mexican grandmother, author, and founder of orders of priests, sisters, and laypeople. *31*

de Bragança, Nadejda (d. 1946). Portuguese-American poet. *82*

de Chantal, Jeanne Frances (1572–1641). French noblewoman and mystic who founded the Sisters of Visitation, and was canonized in 1751. *54*

Dickinson, Emily (1830–1886). American poet. *15*

Eliot, George (1819–1880). English novelist. *80*

Elliot, Julia A. (d. 1841). Hymn writer. *45*

Elliott, Charlotte (1789–1871). English hymn writer famous for "Just As I Am." *50, 62*

Evans, Laura Margaret (20th century). Writer and mother of three daughters. *57*

Findley, Kathy Manis (20th century). Pastor and chaplain associate in Little Rock, Arkansas. *33, 94*

Fry, Elizabeth (1780–1845). Quaker and reformer of British prison system. *76, 80*

Galgani, Gemma (1878–1903). Italian saint canonized in 1940. *70*

Garrison, Theodosia (1874–1944). American poet. *76*

Gertrude the Great (1256–1302). German mystic, writer, and leader at the Benedictine monastery at Helfta. *13, 16, 84*

Gilman, Charlotte Perkins (1860–1935). American social critic and author of fiction and nonfiction. *41*

Goforth, Rosalind (1864–1942). Canadian missionary to China who (along with her husband Jonathan) was severely wounded during the Boxer Rebellion of 1900. Together the couple contributed to revival in Korea in 1907 and later returned to work in China. *98*

Goudge, Elizabeth (1900–1984). English novelist and writer of poetry and prose. *42*

Graham, Ruth Bell (20th century). American author; wife of evangelist Billy Graham. *21, 34*

Greig, Doris W. (20th century). No information available. *70*

Grey, Lady Jane (1537–1554). Great-granddaughter of King Henry VII of England. She was charged with treason and beheaded. *20*

Griffiths, Ann (18th century). Welsh hymn writer. *59*

Grimes, Emily May (1868–1927). Hymn writer. *12*

Guyon, Madame Jeanne (1648–1717). French mystic and writer who was imprisoned and later banished by the church for her Quietist views. *14, 25, 61, 70, 92, 122, 127*

Haley, Molly Anderson (b. 1888). No information available. *82*

Hare, Maria (1807–1870). English writer of prayers that are still widely used today. *98*

Harkness, Georgia (1891–1974). Theologian, teacher, and Methodist minister. Author of *Prayer and the Common Life* and *Women in Church and Society.* *41*

Harrell, Irene Burk (20th century). Homemaker and writer of books and articles. *121*

Havergal, Frances Ridley (1836–1879). English poet and hymn writer. *22, 62, 88, 128, 133*

Head, Bessie P. (1850–1936). Hymn writer. *99*

Heald, Cynthia (20th century). Staff member with the Navigators ministry, author of several books, including *Becoming a Woman of Prayer.* *16, 26, 36, 60*

Heard, Josephine Delphine Henderson (1861–1921). African-American teacher and poet. *134*

Heidebrecht, Priscilla (20th century). ESL (English as a second language) teacher and mother of three. *76, 96*

Hemans, Felicia Dorothea (1794–1835). English poet and translator. *14*

Herklots, Rosamond E. (20th century). English hymn writer born in India. *46*

Hildegard of Bingen (1098–1179). Benedictine nun and visionary famous for her scholarly works. *25, 117, 122*

Hillesum, Etty (d. 1943). Young woman of Dutch Jewish ancestry who left wartime diaries, partly published in *An Interrupted Life,* revealing her faith under the extreme conditions of Nazi occupation and imprisonment. *82, 83, 126*

Holmes, Marjorie (20th century). Poetry, fiction, and devotional writer. *12*

Holtby, Winifred (1898–1935). English novelist, author of *South Riding*. *74*

Hong, Edna Hatlestad (20th century). Writer of books and poetry, mother of eight, co-translator of works of Søren Kierkegaard. *29, 37*

Howard, Katherine G. (1899–1987). Mother of Elisabeth Elliot. *86*

Huntington, Lady (1707–1791). English countess and patroness of revivalist George Whitfield and the Methodist movement. *71, 135*

Hurnard, Hannah (1905–1990). Author of *Hind's Feet on High Places* and missionary. *113*

Hybels, Lynne (20th century). Author, speaker, and wife of Bill Hybels of Willow Creek Church. *108*

Hyde, Abby Bradley (1799–1872). American hymn writer. *82*

Ileana of Romania, Princess (20th century). Great-granddaughter of Queen Victoria and daughter of King Ferdinand of Romania. *35*

Jordan-Lake, Joy (20th century). American writer. *81*

Julian of Norwich (c. 1342–1413). Benedictine nun and mystic. *15*

Keith, Anne (1915–1994). American poet. *63*

Kelly, Sister (19th century). Ex-slave who became a washerwoman in Nashville, Tennessee, after the Civil War. *126*

Kempe, Margery (c. 1373–c. 1438). Originator of the first autobiography in English, dictated to a priest because she was illiterate. *23, 91*

Killinger, Anne (20th century). Homemaker, writer, and pianist. *55*

Kimball, Harriet McEwen (b. 1834). Poet. *34, 74*

Kjos, Berit (20th century). Conference speaker and author of *Brave New Schools* and *Your Child and the New Age*. *97*

Kuhn, Isobel (1901–1957). American missionary to China. *111*

Larson, Elizabeth (20th century). No information available. *60*

Lathbury, Mary Artemisia (1841–1913). American poet and author of children's books. *44, 56*

Lee, Susan Hagood (20th century). American Episcopal priest. *88*

L'Engle, Madeleine (20th century). American author and recipient of the American Book Award and the Newbery Award for young adult fiction. *45, 106*

Leseur, Elisabeth (1866–1914). Upper-class French woman who lived a life of Christian devotion which she recorded in her diary. Her atheist husband was converted after reading the diary and later became a priest. *12, 93*

Levertov, Denise (20th century). English-born poet, now an American citizen. Her work is frequently anthologized. *64*

Lim, Poh Lian (20th century). Malaysian-born medical doctor who works at a Boston area community health center serving primarily Asian immigrants and refugees. *59*

Lindbergh, Anne Morrow (1906–1955). Writer, wife of Charles Lindbergh. *73*

Livingstone, Mary (19th century). Wife of David Livingstone, explorer of Africa and missionary. *99*

Love, Dreama Plybon (20th century). Single parent and education program director for a child advocacy organization. *28, 31, 112*

Lucas, Alice. No information available. *41*

Ludamilia Elisabeth (1640–1672). Countess of Schwarzburg. *55*

Macleod, Fiona (1855–1905). Surprise—she's really William Sharp (Fiona is his pen name). It's a beautiful prayer so we left it in. *35*

Mains, Karen Burton (20th century). American writer and speaker. *23, 58, 122*

Mansfield, Katherine (1888–1923). New Zealand-born English author. *43*

Maritain, Raissa (1883–1960). Russian-born contemplative, writer, and wife of French philosopher Jacques Maritain. *79, 118*

Marshall, Catherine (1915–1983). American author and wife of former U.S. Senate chaplain Peter Marshall. *27, 107, 117*

Mary Stuart, Queen of Scotland (1542–1587). Roman Catholic queen, imprisoned by Queen Elizabeth for nineteen years and then beheaded. *105*

Maude, Mary Fawler (1820–1913). English poet and author of books on customs and manners in Scriptures. *28*

Mayhall, Carole (20th century). American writer and speaker. *27, 111*

Mears, Henrietta (1890–1963). A noted Bible teacher, she was Christian education director at First Presbyterian Church of Hollywood, California, and founded Gospel Light Publications and Forest Home Christian Conference Center. *102*

Mechtild of Magdeburg (1210–1294). German Benedictine mystic. *63, 64*

Millay, Edna Saint Vincent (1892–1950). American poet, winner of the Pulitzer Prize in 1923. *65*

Miller, Rose Marie (20th century). Church planter with World Harvest Mission. *54, 111*

Mindeman, Miriam (20th century). Mother of two, teacher, editor. *70*

Mistral, Gabriela (1889–1957). Chilean poet, winner of the Nobel Prize for Literature in 1946. *73*

Moon, Lottie (Charlotte) (1840–1912). American missionary to China. *26*

Moore, Pamela Rosewell (20th century). English author and speaker who assisted Brother Andrew for seven years in his ministry to Christians behind the Iron Curtain and served as Corrie ten Boom's companion for the last seven years of her life. *100*

More, Hannah (1745–1833). British writer of dramas and tracts. *86*

Morris, Margaret Hill (18th century). Quaker in colonial America. *94*

Nightingale, Florence (1820–1910). English nurse considered the founder of modern nursing. *79*

Ortlund, Anne (20th century). American writer and speaker. *125*

Owen, Frances (1842–1883). No information available. *43*

Palmer, Phoebe (19th century). Member of the Methodist movement. *124*

Paris, Twila (20th century). Contemporary Christian singer-songwriter. *47, 71*

Pigott, Jean Sophia (1845–1882). Hymn writer. *41, 100*

Phillips, Harriett C. (1806–1884). American hymn writer. *125*

Pollard, Adelaide A. (1862–1934). Hymn writer. *102*

Powers, Jessica (1905-1988). American Carmelite nun and poet. *72-73*

Prentiss, Elizabeth P. (1818–1878). American hymn writer, poet, and schoolteacher. *74, 120*

Price, Eugenia (20th century). American author. *108*

Procter, Adelaide Anne (1825–1864). English poet and follower of John Henry Newman. *127*

Richardson, Ruth (20th century). Credit analyst completing a graduate degree in written communication. *24, 133*

Robertson, Josephine (20th century). Devotional writer. *35, 83, 130*

Rooney, Elizabeth (20th century). American poet. *93, 109*

Rossetti, Christina (1830–1894). Anglican poet. *12, 22, 30, 54, 56, 59, 84, 98, 101, 117*

Rowe, Elizabeth Singer (1674–1737). British hymn writer, poet, and philanthropist. *44, 86, 116, 129*

Rowlandson, Mary (c. 1637–1711). Early American settler kept for nearly twelve weeks as a captive of the Narragansett Indians. *126*

Sanford, Agnes (20th century). Author, speaker, and practitioner of a church-based healing ministry. *47*

Sangster, Margaret E. (1838–1912). Poet, novelist, editor of *Harper's Bazaar. 58, 83*

Schaefer, Sister M. Cherubim (20th century). Educator and composer. *129*

Schaeffer, Edith (20th century). American writer and speaker. *22, 44, 92, 107*

Scott, Caroline (20th century). Manager, insurance firm. *69*

Scott, Elizabeth (c. 1708–c. 1776). English-born American hymnwriter. *134*

Seton, Elizabeth (1774–1821). American religious leader who founded the Sisters of Charity and was the first native-born American to be canonized. *16, 99*

Shaw, Luci (20th century). American poet. *30, 40, 41, 99, 110, 118, 128*

Shirreff, Emily L. (1814–1897). Hymn writer. *80*

Simms, Florence (1873–1923). American leader of the YWCA and advocate for better working conditions for women. *83*

Skobtsova, Mother Maria (1891–c. 1945). Russian-born Russian-Orthodox nun in Northern France, probably died in gas chambers. *43*

Slessor, Mary (1848–1915). Missionary to Calabar, Nigeria. *21, 101*

Smith, Amanda (1837–1915). African-American evangelist. *27, 112*

Smith, Hannah Whitall (1832–1911). American Quaker and author of *The Christian's Secret of a Happy Life. 15, 28, 49, 102*

Sook, Ahn Ei (20th century). Survivor of six years' imprisonment (1939–1945) for attempting to plead before the Japanese government the case of fellow Korean Christians imprisoned and tortured by the Japanese. *93*

Stapleton, Ruth Carter (20th century). Evangelist, author, and sister of former president Jimmy Carter. *62*

Steele, Anne (1716–1778). England's first woman to have hymns published. *42*

Stevenson, Isabella S. (1843–1890). Hymn writer. *84*

Stewart, Elsa L. (20th century) Creator, Glad Heart Originals. *121, 133*

Stewart, Maria W. (1803–1879). First black woman to speak out for black advancement, and earliest American woman whose public speeches are still in print. *49*

Stewart, Mary (1878–1943). American superintendent of education for the Native Americans of California. *64-65, 79*

Storey, Violet Alleyn (20th century). American poet. *68, 90*

Stowe, Harriet Beecher (1811–1896). American author of *Uncle Tom's Cabin. 34, 60, 65*

Strubel, Deborah (20th century). Writer, editor, and mother. *121*

Sumner, Mary (1828–1921). Founder of a Christian Mother's Union in England. *86*

Teichner, Miriam (b.1888). American poet and journalist. *70*

ten Boom, Corrie (1893–1983). Inspirational writer and speaker from Holland who survived a concentration camp in World War II. *46, 101, 109*

Teresa of Avila (1515–1582). Spanish saint and mystic, and reformer of the Order of Carmelites. *46, 51, 85, 98, 101, 104, 131*

Teresa of Calcutta, Mother (1910–1997). Albanian-born Indian nun and winner of the 1979 Nobel Peace Prize; founder of the Sisters of Charity. *22, 72, 74, 78, 91, 119*

Thérèse of Lisieux (1873–1897). French Carmelite nun and author of the spiritual classic *The Story of a Soul. 34, 100, 120*

Thomson, Mary A. (1834–1923). English born American poet and hymn writer. *132*

Trimmer, Sarah Kirby (1741–1810). English author and advocate for education. *29*

Trimiew, Anna (20th century). Freelance writer. *13, 32, 124*

Troccoli, Kathy (20th century). Contemporary Christian singer-songwriter. *82*

Trotter, Lilias (1853–1928). Pioneer missionary to Muslim North Africa. *90, 96*

Truth, Sojourner (c. 1797–1883). American preacher and activist in the antislavery movement and rights for women. *104, 108*

Tsai, Christiana (1890–1984). Chinese Christian who fled China during the Japanese invasion and supported training of Chinese Christians through Ambassadors for Christ. *51*

Tubman, Harriet (c. 1820–1913). American fugitive slave active in the Underground Railroad, which lead slaves to freedom before and during the Civil War. *55*

Underhill, Evelyn (1875–1941). Modern English mystic, poet, novelist, and scholar of mysticism. *13, 65, 85*

Vidakovich, Mary Anna (20th century). United Methodist pastor in Illinois. *20, 73*

von Bora, Katherine (1499–1552). Wife of German Reformer Martin Luther. *79*

von Speyr, Adrienne (1902–1967). Swiss physician, Catholic convert, mystic, and writer. *48, 68, 89*

von Tiele-Winckler, Eva (1866–1930). From a wealthy Prussian family, founded a deaconess movement, evangelizing and serving the most needy. *97*

Wang, Mary (20th century). Chinese author who escaped Communist persecution by fleeing to Hong Kong and then England. *21*

Ward, Mary (1585–1645). English founder of a religious congregation modeled on the Jesuit order. She spent most of her life in Europe. *50*

Warde, Frances (1810–1884). Founder of the Sisters of Mercy in the U.S. *32*

Waring, Anna L. (1820–1910). Welsh poet and hymn writer. *71*

Wenger, Miriam (20th century). Mennonite missionary who went to East Africa with her husband in the late 1930s. *17*

Wesley, Susanna (1669–1742). Devoted mother of nineteen children, including John and Charles Wesley, the founders of Methodism. *36, 56, 107*

Whitmell, Lucy (20th century). Poet. *59*

Wilkinson, Marguerite (1883–1928), Lecturer and poetry reviewer, born in Canada and raised in the U.S. *63*